A SEASON TO REMEMBER

BRISTOL ROVERS'
PROMOTION SEASON 1973/74

A SEASON TO REMEMBER

BRISTOL ROVERS' PROMOTION SEASON 1973/74

IAN HADDRELL & MIKE JAY

The
History
Press

First published 2010

Reprinted in 2011

The History Press
The Mill, Brimscombe Port
Stroud, Gloucestershire, GL5 2QG
www.thehistorypress.co.uk

© Ian Haddrell and Mike Jay, 2011

The right of Ian Haddrell and Mike Jay to be identified as the Author
of this work has been asserted in accordance with the
Copyrights, Designs and Patents Act 1988.

British Library Cataloguing in Publication Data.
A catalogue record for this book is available from the British Library.

ISBN 978 0 7524 5832 8

Typesetting and origination by The History Press
Printed and bound in Great Britain by
Marston Book Services Limited, Didcot, Oxon

CONTENTS

ACKNOWLEDGEMENTS

Bristol Evening Post; Bristol Rovers Football Club; Bristol Rovers Supporters' Club; Keith Brookman; Chris Brown; Stephen Byrne; Bob Coyne; Graham Day; Herbert Gillam; Peter Godsiff; Phil Greig Photography of Stoke; Stephen Halliday; Nick Harris; Lee Honeyball; Colin Howlett; *The Independent*; Wayne Jones; John Kelland; Mark Leesdad; Phil McCheyne Photography of Nailsea; *Observer Sport Monthly*; *The Observer*; Robin Perry; *The Scotsman*; Greg Stock; *Soccer History*; David Solomons; Stoke City Football Club; *The Sunday Times*; Torquay United Football Club; Rick Weston; *Western Daily Press*; Andre Zlotkowski.

Our grateful thanks are extended to Alan Marshall, Bristol Rovers' official photographer from 1973 to 2006, for giving permission to use pictures from his vast photographic collection. Every effort has been made to identify copyright holders of illustrations from published materials, but the authors apologise to anyone overlooked in our search, or to photograph owners, should their names be omitted from the above list.

A special thank you to Don Megson and all the players for their magnificent efforts during the 1973/74 season, as well as their contributions and help in producing this record of a memorable period in the proud history of Bristol Rovers Football Club.

This book is intended as a comprehensive record of Bristol Rovers' successful 1973/74 season, compiled from contemporary newspaper reports, published sources, match-day programmes – there's nothing more evocative than an old football programme – together with players' and fans' personal recollections. It is hoped that through the pages and pictures this volume will revive those exciting, historic moments which helped take Bristol Rovers back to Division Two, for those who witnessed the events, and act as a point of reference for those Rovers fans who are too young to understand what all the fuss was about.

FOREWORD

I would like to thank Ian and Mike for giving me the opportunity to contribute to what I hope will give an insight into the fantastic promotion season of 1973/74, and will also document a few of my own memories of my time at Bristol Rovers.

My career at Sheffield Wednesday had come to its end, having played for ten years in the First Division (now the Premier League), and it came as a bit of a culture shock when I arrived in Bristol. Not being snobby, but the hotel the club had booked for me was awful, so I went and booked myself into the Grand Hotel, and when Bill Dodgin came to take me to the game at Eastville, we went on the bus. Not the preparation I had been used to! The club had been in the Third Division for eight years, but there was a really strong drive to get into the Second Division which I liked. However, for that to happen the thinking would have to change dramatically.

I played thirty odd games for Rovers before injury ended my playing career, and I became Bill Dodgin's assistant, though this had its problems. Getting on with Bill off the pitch was fine, but we had different ideas about preparing a team for matches. With his guidance I was given the reserve team to learn management skills, for which I will always be grateful.

After being made manager, at my first board meeting my only brief was, 'Just get us out of this division, we have been here far too long'. Bill had left me with a decent team, which scored lots of goals, but also let a lot in. All managers will tell you that to play fast, entertaining football and *win* is the ideal way, but that is easier said than done, so I decided to pay more attention to making us harder to beat by preparing better defensively. Much later on, this did not endear me to the folks who liked Bill's style, but we won the Watney Cup early on in my first season in charge and this laid the foundation for the future.

1973/74 was for me and the players the most rewarding season in our time with Rovers, as we went thirty-odd games without losing and this book will tell you in detail all about our journey. I had now put my own stamp on the squad, and the team mainly made up of: Jim Eadie, our 'Dennis the Menace', who marched to his own drum; Trevor Jacobs, Lindsay Parsons, Tom Stanton and Frankie Prince, who were my unsung heroes, which every good team needs – win it, give it, fight all day, they did that so many times; Big Stuart Taylor at 6ft 5in was there to take care of high stuff, with Mike Green, the thinking man's sweeper and anchorman; Kenny Stephens, wide right on the wing, with Colin Dobson, on the left wing but playing deeper, provided the opportunities for big Alan Warboys and Bruce Bannister to score forty-odd goals between them. Add to that the desire to win, the mental strength to fight all day, the 'over-my-dead-body' attitude to keep a clean sheet, and an 'over-the-90-minutes-we-will-get-at-least-one-goal-in-your-net' approach, and you have a promotion team.

Two sayings are often used in football. One is 'The ups and downs of football' while the other one is 'They can't take your memories away'. The ups for me were, obviously, the Watney Cup and promotion, plus many, many more. The downs were the disappointments: the passing of Bert Tann so soon after I took over as manager; the loss of Wayne Jones to arthritic knees; Andrew Evans, a twenty-year-old left winger we had really high hopes of possibly becoming the Ryan Giggs of his time, but his ankle was shattered so badly that he never played again; Dick Sheppard received a fractured skull diving at the feet of an opposition forward and lost a brave fight in his efforts to play again. All these things have stayed with me to this day. On the club side of things, my biggest disappointment was the fact that we didn't strengthen the team after we were promoted;

in fact, we lost the likes of Alan Warboys, Bruce Bannister and Mike Green because of the lack of finances. We missed a great chance to push on. My best and proudest moment came when we gained promotion at Southend, with all our supporters on the pitch cheering to the rooftops. We were all stood in the Directors' Box when I remembered Bill's part in getting us there and I went down to their boardroom, brought him up and raised his hand to tremendous cheers. It really was a magic moment.

On the social side, my wife Yvonne and I had some fantastic times with some wonderful friends, Doug Hillard and his wife, Janet, and John Ferris and his wife, Janette, being our closest, together with many, many more who made our stay in Bristol so memorable. I hope you enjoy the book.

Thanks for the memories,
Yours in sport,

Don Megson
Manager, Bristol Rovers FC 1972-1977

INTRODUCTION

I imagine that every person who supports a football team over a long period has a favourite era, group of players, season or event while following their chosen team that is more remarkable, memorable or special for them to obsess about. For some Rovers' supporters it may be the 1989/90 promotion season when the Pirates went up as champions of the Third Division, pipping their local rivals to the top spot, together with a first-ever Wembley appearance in the Leyland Daf Trophy Final against Tranmere Rovers. This was the extraordinary achievement for Gerry Francis' 'Ragbag Rovers' at their temporary home at Twerton Park in Bath. For others, it may be the 2006/07 season with appearances at the Millennium Stadium and Wembley in the same year – emulating the FA and League Cup winners Chelsea – culminating in Sammy Igoe's late wonder goal to secure promotion in the final seconds of the season. There will also be those who recall the legendary 1952/53 Third Division South championship team.

There may have been more significant occasions in Rovers' long history, but the late Sixties and early Seventies is 'my era', with Rovers' progression in successive League Cup competitions, triumph in the Watney Cup and promotion to the Second Division providing some treasured footballing memories of that period. The League Cup runs are memorable, not only for the results achieved against sides from higher divisions, but also for the incredible atmosphere generated by large crowds under the Eastville floodlights on cold winter evenings – with a distinctive aroma drifting across the ground! Standing on the Tote End as an impressionable teenager, watching momentous League Cup ties against Newcastle United, Birmingham City, Norwich City, Manchester United, Aston Villa and Stoke City, and, of course, the Watney Cup triumph against Sheffield United at the start of the 1972/1973 season, have left enduring memories of those remarkable times at Eastville.

The previous season's Watney Cup victory and the reintroduction of the famous quartered shirts in the summer of 1973 gave me a sense of anticipation, almost excitement, at the start of the new season. As the campaign began and the unbeaten League run started to take shape, a significant game for me was the visit to Blackburn Rovers, a club with a long and successful history who were considered strong promotion rivals. But the 2-0 away victory brought a belief that this might just be Rovers' year. Anyone who, as I did, shared the elation of the first two-thirds of the season and the trauma of the final third, will never forget those scenes at Southend after 'Megson's Marvels' gained the point needed to make sure of promotion. It was a long and difficult journey to Southend, and for a Friday night match it meant taking time off work to get to Roots Hall, but along with the 1,000 other Rovers fans who witnessed the game, it was all worthwhile – and a great relief.

Ian Haddrell
November 2010

My own personal memories of the remarkable promotion season are many. Having started to watch Rovers for the first time on April Fool's Day, 1967, besides the tremendous League Cup runs of the early 1970s, this was the first time as a teenager that I was genuinely excited by the team and the prospects of promotion to the Second Division. From the 1968/69 season I had managed to see all the home matches and travelled to a limited number of away games when finances allowed. However, seeing Rovers in those distinctive blue-and-white-quartered shirts for the first time was special. The 1973/74 squad, comprising a number of Bristol-born players and those from the Rovers' youth scheme in South Wales, really established the club in the national headlines as their unbeaten record grew as the season progressed.

For myself there were many highlights. Travelling on the opening day of the season to see the 3-0 victory at Bournemouth was a tremendous boost. The emergence of Bruce Bannister and Alan Warboys as our potent strike force and the way the whole team defended, with Eadie keeping so many clean sheets behind a settled defence of Stuart Taylor, Mike Green, Trevor Jacobs and Lindsay Parsons, who conceded just thirty-three goals, was the cornerstone to achieving promotion. The influence of Frankie Prince, Tommy Stanton and the contribution of the experienced Colin Dobson was significant, but I feel that Dobson did not get the full credit he deserved at the time. The Boxing Day West Country derby defeat of Plymouth at Eastville was, for me, one of the best performances of the season. The novelty of travelling to Aldershot for our first ever Sunday League match due to the national power restrictions and coming away with a 3-2 win was exciting.

One of my big disappointments was the decision not to travel to Brighton for the famous 8-2 win, as it appeared likely the match would be postponed due to frost. I saw the first defeat in thirty-two League matches at Wrexham and remember how the Welsh fans wildly celebrated their team's feat. Other lows were the Easter home defeat by Oldham and the gradual loss of what looked likely to have been the championship. But the fact that promotion was achieved in some style was the overriding joy. The prospect of competing against some of the big clubs in the Second Division, such as Manchester United, West Bromwich Albion, Southampton, Sunderland, Aston Villa and Fulham, and visiting their famous grounds, was intriguing. Plus, the opportunity to resume Bristol derbies after an absence of nine years was certainly well worth looking forward to.

Mike Jay
November 2010

1

LEAGUE CUP SUCCESS

The culmination of several seasons of development into producing a team to eventually gain promotion was started by Bristol Rovers in the early 1970s, following the appointment of Bill Dodgin as manager in August 1969. Dodgin stepped up from chief scout to team manager of Rovers for three years while a younger man could be groomed to take over the job. A combination of older experienced 'pros' and some up-and-coming young professionals, in a team assembled by the ex-Rovers player and former manager of Southampton, Brentford and Fulham, put together some impressive performances; none more so than in the Football League Cup competition.

Bill Dodgin, Bristol Rovers' manager between August 1969 and July 1972.

However, promotion from the then Third Division still occupied everyone's thoughts during 1969/70 and Bill Dodgin was given the luxury of being able to spend to strengthen his squad. He bought inside forward Sandy Allan from Cardiff City for £12,500 and as results continued to improve, the crowds began to return to Eastville Stadium. Everyone wondered if the long-awaited return to the Second Division was now at hand as top-of-the-table Leyton Orient were defeated at the end of March by a Carl Gilbert goal in a 1-0 victory. Hopes were dampened somewhat when the next three games were all drawn, but Rovers were still in with a chance, and the fans were still willing to back them, with 19,040 at Eastville for the match against Doncaster Rovers, while 17,559 fans saw Stockport County beaten 1-0 by a Sandy Allan goal in the next home game. Everything now depended on the last two games of the season – against Gillingham at Eastville and away to Tranmere Rovers. Frustrated Rovers supporters saw their side go down 2-1 at Gillingham and with the side's momentum gone, a 5-2 reverse at Tranmere left Rovers in third place.

Bristol Rovers' most significant new recruit arrived in March 1970 when former Sheffield Wednesday favourite, Don Megson, was signed by team manager Dodgin. Megson, the Owls' captain and left-back, had been a loyal servant to the Hillsborough club for seventeen years and it quickly emerged that he was the man Rovers' board thought could be groomed into the ambitious, young 'tracksuit' manager they eventually wanted to succeed Dodgin. Megson was immediately given the role of player-coach, Dodgin writing at the time that it was a great help to have his assistance on the coaching side as Bobby Campbell and himself had to contend with the coaching, training and treatment of all the playing staff. Making his debut on 28 March in the home victory over League leaders Orient, in front of 22,005 spectators at Eastville, Megson immediately made a major contribution. He gave some fine displays in thirty-one League appearances before deciding to end his playing days and concentrate on coaching at the end of the 1970/71 season.

Heartened by the previous season's success, Rovers approached 1970/71 with vigour and enthusiasm as slowly but surely a team worthy of promotion to Division Two was being constructed. Stuart Taylor, Frankie Prince, Lindsay Parsons and Bryn Jones would all star in the 1973/74 side, and they were joined by two free-transfer recruits, Walsall's Kenny Stephens and Gordon Fearnley, previously a teammate of Don Megson at Sheffield Wednesday. But despite starting the season with an impressive fourteen-match run with only one defeat, Rovers never seriously challenged for a place in the top two. Finishing the season with straight defeats, Dodgin's side had not achieved its pre-season aspirations in terms of League football, finishing in sixth spot, but the League Cup was to provide enormous excitement.

Rovers had been knocked out of the competition in the first round in each of the previous six seasons, so there was considerable satisfaction when Second Division Brighton were beaten 1-0 at Eastville by a Ray Graydon goal in the opening round of 1970/71. Rovers drew First Division Newcastle United in the second round, and the 16,824 spectators who attended were hoping for something special from this match. They were not let down, as two goals from veteran Bobby Jones ensured a well-merited 2-1 home triumph.

Norwich City away, another Second Division club, was the next hurdle and Rovers held them to a 1-1 draw at Carrow Road, Bobby Jones again scoring the vital goal that earned a replay. The Eastville game went into extra time, finishing 1-1 after 90 minutes, but Rovers' stamina in the energy-sapping additional half-hour saw them through to a 3-1 victory, with Don Megson putting them ahead with his first goal for the club.

Supporters were really beginning to smell the scent of Cup success, and this was reflected in the attendances. There had been 19,122 at the Norwich replay and for the fourth-round tie, at home to Birmingham City, 22,189 excited fans were in the ground. An own goal from Birmingham's centre half Roger Hynd and goals from Carl Gilbert and Robin Stubbs allowed Rovers to cruise to their third win against Second Division clubs in the season's competition. In the quarter-final Rovers were paired with promotion rivals Aston Villa at Eastville and, despite torrential rain, 28,780 spectators packed the ground. The weather won though, spoiling the game both as a spectacle and test of skill, and a 1-1 draw, with Stuart Taylor scoring for Rovers, was a fair result. The replay, eight days later, attracted an even larger crowd − 36,482, remarkable for two Third Division teams − and this time they saw an outstanding match. Play flowed from end to end and Villa Park was alive with excitement, as both teams tried to break the 0-0 deadlock. With virtually the last kick of the game, Villa won the tie with a Pat McMahon goal to take the Midlanders into the semi-final, where they triumphed against Manchester United before losing to Spurs in the final.

Rovers set out on the 1971/72 campaign with a similar staff as the previous season. The main absentee was Ray Graydon, who was sold to Aston Villa in exchange for the highly experienced former Welsh international Brian Godfrey, while Mike Green appeared in the side following his

Bobby Jones heads in the first of his two goals for Rovers against First Division Newcastle United.

Don Megson shoots Rovers ahead in extra time against Norwich City at Eastville, 13 October 1970.

Harold Jarman volleys in Rovers' first goal in the 3-1 third-round victory over Sunderland.

Sandy Allan makes amends for his missed penalty as he races through the QPR defence to score Rovers' winning goal.

move from Gillingham and Malcolm John made his League debut. Another product of the South Wales nursery organised by Stan Montgomery, seventeen-year-old Peter Aitken, made his way into the squad as an unused substitute. A significant change of career was that of Don Megson, who retired as a player to concentrate on his full-time role as a coach. It is surprising how similar the results achieved were compared with the previous season – another good spell in the League Cup culminating in another quarter-final appearance, and an identical final placing of sixth in the Third Division. The League Cup run started with a comparatively straight-forward 3-0 away win against Exeter City, earning Rovers the right to entertain Sunderland at Eastville in the second round. Rovers disposed of them almost as nonchalantly, winning 3-1 with goals from Harold Jarman, Wayne Jones and Sandy Allan, and then put pay to Charlton Athletic, another Second Division club, in round three, this time 2-1 with Jarman and Stuart Taylor the goalscorers.

Excitement in Bristol built up quickly after Rovers drew 1-1 away to Queens Park Rangers in the next round, and there was a 24,373 crowd at Eastville for the replay when Rovers, for the second season running, defeated their third set of Second Division opponents, Sandy Allan scoring the only goal of a thrilling match 12 minutes from time, having missed an earlier penalty.

Stoke City at home was the quarter-final draw, a crowd-pulling fixture as the First Division Potteries' star-studded side included Gordon Banks, one of the 1966 World Cup winners and believed by many to be the greatest goalkeeper in the world. The 33,624 attendance was Rovers' record for a home League Cup tie. Banks was kept busy in the opening half-hour, but then Stoke settled down to serve up some top-class football with George Eastham, playing with the aplomb of an ageing soccer aristocrat, mesmerising everyone with his skill. Stoke ran up a convincing four-goal lead but relaxed too early, which enabled Robin Stubbs and a Brian Godfrey penalty to make

Stoke City's England goalkeeper Gordon Banks hugs the ball to his body as Robin Stubbs and Bobby Jones move in to challenge.

the final scoreline respectable at 4-2. Stoke went on to reach the last stage of the competition, beating Chelsea 2-1 in a Wembley final.

Anxious to boost the bid for Second Division status, manager Dodgin broke Rovers' transfer record in November 1971 when he paid a £23,000 fee to secure Bradford City's top goal-poacher Bruce Bannister. In the following March he let Robin Stubbs, who had scored only twice in fifteen full appearances plus three as substitute during the season, return to Torquay United in exchange for another forward, the experienced John Rudge. After a few initial concerns in the League, Rovers put together some good sequences of results, notably between November and February when they went on a nine-match unbeaten run. At last Rovers had found something approaching promotion form. With a run of successive wins over Mansfield Town, Blackburn Rovers, Tranmere Rovers, Oldham Athletic and Blackburn Rovers again, followed by a 0-0 draw at Port Vale, they surged into a challenging position. The 'crunch' match was the Easter Monday visit to League leaders Aston Villa, but in front of 41,518 fans Rovers unfortunately lost 2-1 and, as they obtained only two points from their next four games, the Eastville fans had to watch Villa and Brighton take the top two positions in the division as Rovers remained in fifth place.

In July 1972, Bill Dodgin handed over the reigns of management to Don Megson, with Bill reverting to the post of chief scout. Disappointed though he may have been that the main prizes had slipped from his grasp – as they always had throughout his managerial career – Dodgin had done a good job in building a Rovers side capable of challenging for promotion. The club had enjoyed their best three seasons for years in the League, and even more so in the League Cup competition. Dodgin had been responsible for some judicious transfers, both incoming and outgoing, and at the same time the young players were maturing. Now he had to seek his satisfaction again as a 'backroom boy' for the twilight of his distinguished career, helping spot and groom the stars of tomorrow, while a younger manager wrestled with the daily challenge of steering the club's overall affairs. Dodgin held the position of chief scout until 1983, when he retired at the age of seventy-two.

At thirty-six, Megson, the Sale-born former Sheffield Wednesday captain and full-back, had displayed considerable talent as a player and it was hoped he could translate his expertise into good management; as events transpired, Rovers were not to be disappointed. In the summer of 1972, Megson made just one major signing, procuring his former Sheffield Wednesday colleague and erstwhile England Under-23 international winger Colin Dobson on a free transfer as player-coach. This was the first of a number of astute acquisitions he made to ensure that Rovers would be serious promotion contenders in 1973/74.

2

WATNEY CUP TRIUMPH

The League Cup has gone through five name changes since the Milk Board first put their name on the trophy in 1982. Now known as the Carling Cup, it is not, however, the first competition to adopt its sponsor's name. That honour goes to a pre-season event called the Watney Mann Invitation Cup, which lasted four seasons from 1970. In the autumn of 1969 Watneys and the Football League persuaded the Football Association to change its regulations to allow sponsorship of professional football for the first time in England, and the Watney Cup was born. The brewery sponsored the innovative knockout competition between eight teams, two from each of the four divisions, entry being awarded to clubs who scored the most goals in their division the previous season but were not promoted or didn't qualify to play in Europe. It was a one-leg knockout. If the sides were level at full-time, they went to a penalty shoot-out, the first time it had been used in professional football in England. Manchester United's George Best was the first player to score from the spot, against Hull in 1970, and teammate Denis Law was the first to miss. In the first season of the Watney Cup, Rovers failed to qualify by just one goal; the second season, they were three goals short of a place in the competition. Don Megson's managerial ability was certainly to be tested early, as the 1972 pre-season Watney Cup paired Rovers with First Division

Wolves' new £100,000 forward Steve Kindon takes on Rovers' full-back Phil Roberts during the 1972 Watney Cup first-round tie.

Wolverhampton Wanderers at Eastville. It was a hurdle that was cleared with almost surprising ease, as Rovers won 2-0 with Bruce Bannister (penalty) and Kenny Stephens scoring.

Burnley away, midweek, was the next match and again Rovers won 2-0, in front of 10,589 fans. This time the marksmen were Frankie Prince and Bruce Bannister, and the true merit of this victory was underlined when Burnley proceeded to win the Second Division championship that season. So Third Division Bristol Rovers reached the Watney Cup Final. Their opponents were First Division Sheffield United and a crowd of 19,768 were at Eastville on one of the hottest days of the year to see if Don Megson could pilot the club to its first national cup triumph in its eighty-nine-years existence. It was only his third game in charge.

SATURDAY 5 AUGUST 1972, EASTVILLE STADIUM

Bristol Rovers	0
Sheffield United	0
Half-time:	0-0
Attendance:	19,768
Referee:	John Yates (Redditch)
Bristol Rovers:	Sheppard, Roberts, Parsons, Green, Taylor, Prince, Stephens, Jones (W), Allan, Bannister, Godfrey. Substitutes: Jones (B) for Prince, Dalrymple, Fearnley, Jarman, Stanton
Sheffield United:	McAlister, Goulding, Hemsley, MacKenzie, Colquhoun, Hockey, Woodward, Salmons, Deardon, Currie, Scullion. Substitute: Eddy for Scullion

Sheffield United enjoyed the midfield skills of England international Tony Currie and a dangerous forward line, which included Alan Woodward and Billy Deardon, but they found their way barred by a well-marshalled Rovers defence, led by Stuart Taylor. At the other end, goalkeeper Tom McAlister had to make three brave saves to deny the home side and it was only his superb goalkeeping which kept the score to 0-0 at the end of an exciting, thrill-packed televised match. McAlister was to make thirteen appearances for Rovers during the 1980/81 season whilst on loan from Swindon Town.

Winger Kenny Stephens evades the challenge of Sheffield United's Welsh international Trevor Hockey.

Rovers players pose with the Watney Cup, the trophy they worked so hard for. From left to right: Campbell (trainer), Roberts, Parsons, Sheppard, Green, Prince, Stephens, Dalyrymple, Fearnley, Stanton, Godfrey. Wayne Jones is in the front.

Tempers became frayed and Stephens and Allan (Rovers) and Trevor Hockey (United) were booked, yet there were no goals – ironically, since the competition was for top-scoring teams – and the game went to penalties. 'We did not practice penalties and after the first five, there weren't people queuing up to take them', remembers centre half Stuart Taylor. In the first round of five penalties for each side, Roberts, Godfrey, Green, Bannister and Allan scored for Rovers; Woodward, Eddy, Currie, Deardon and Colquhoun replied for United, although it took Currie two attempts as Sheppard saved his first effort, but the Rovers goalkeeper was adjudged to have moved before the kick was taken. Now it was 'sudden death'. Parsons scored for Rovers, then Scullion levelled the scores again. Bryn Jones edged Rovers ahead once more and up stepped United's full-back, Ted Hemsley, the Worcestershire cricketer. Hemsley struck the ball to Dick Sheppard's left but the 'keeper got down to smother the ball, enabling Rovers to win the tie-breaking penalty contest 7-6 and give manager Don Megson a fine start to his new job. Rovers' fans celebrated a rare trophy, which was presented to winning captain Brian Godfrey by former athlete Dr Roger Bannister, Chairman of the Sports Council. Megson had won a cup five weeks since gaining his first managerial appointment and after only three games in charge.

'Don Megson came in as the new manager and shored up the defence', recalled defender Taylor. 'Those were the days when we would score eighty goals in a season but let in 120 at the other end'. Bruce Bannister also has fond memories: 'It was a good way to prepare for the season', he says, 'It was not the be-all-and-end-all but there was an edge to the competition that was not there in other pre-season friendlies'.

Dick Sheppard, hero of the penalty shoot-out, proudly holds the Watney Cup

Rovers' captain, Brian Godfrey, scores the first goal against Cardiff City with a powerful left-footed drive.

Tom Stanton taps in the fourth goal to complete a 4-0 second-round win against Brighton.

Rovers thus commenced their 1972/73 League programme cock-a-hoop. With their appetite for glory whetted by the Watney Cup success, the players quickly became engrossed in another spectacular giant-killing run in the League Cup – for the third season in succession. It began with a 2-2 draw away to Second Division Cardiff City. In the replay at Eastville, the Ninian Park club were comfortably beaten 3-1 and then a resounding 4-0 second-round win over Brighton, the team that only four months earlier had pipped Rovers for promotion to Division Two, brought a lucrative home tie against Manchester United.

The famous United team – which included George Best, arguably the most talented British footballer of all time – attracted 33,597 fans to Eastville, but it was Rovers who attracted most of the crowd's cheers as John Rudge's 60th-minute goal earned them a deserved 1-1 draw.

In the replay at Old Trafford eight days later, the team gave what must have been their best away display in the League Cup since the competition was introduced in 1960. There was no fluke about their 2-1 victory, John Rudge again getting his name on the scoresheet, along with Bruce Bannister.

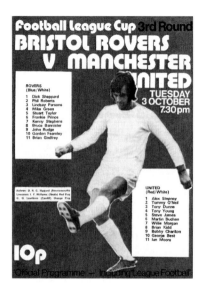

John Rudge scores Rovers' goal against Manchester United in the League Cup tie at Eastville.

Manchester United goalkeeper Alex Stepney parries Brian Godfrey's drive . . .

. . . John Rudge, left follows up to force the ball into the net . . .

. . . and Bruce Bannister raises his arm in jubilation at Rovers' goal.

Celebration time in the Old Trafford dressing room following the 2-1 victory against Manchester United.
From left to right: Lindsay Parsons, Kenny Stephens, Phil Roberts, Frankie Prince, Stuart Taylor, John
Rudge, Wayne Jones, Bobby Campbell, Bobby Jones.

WEDNESDAY 11 OCTOBER 1972, OLD TRAFFORD, MANCHESTER

Manchester United	1 – McIlroy
Bristol Rovers	2 – Rudge, Bannister
Half-time:	0-1
Attendance:	29,349
Referee:	Vince James (York)
Manchester United:	Stepney, Watson, Dunne, Young, James, Buchan, Morgan, Best, Charlton, Kidd, Storey-Moore. Substitute: McIlroy for Kidd (72 mins)
Bristol Rovers:	Sheppard, Roberts, Parsons, Prince, Taylor, Godfrey, Stephens, Jones (W), Rudge, Bannister, Jones (R). Substitute: Green

Rovers' manager surprised everyone by recalling thirty-three-year-old veteran Bobby Jones for the
League Cup third-round replay against Manchester United at Old Trafford. Although United had
avoided defeat at Eastville with an 87th-minute goal from Willie Morgan, few people gave Rovers
a chance in the replay against a team containing nine full internationals. However, Rovers were
undaunted and took the game to United with some splendid attacking football. Goalkeeper Dick
Sheppard dealt competently with several long-range efforts from Bobby Charlton, who failed to
celebrate his thirty-fifth birthday with a goal. It was Rovers who opened the scoring after half an
hour, when Lindsay Parsons swung over a corner from the left and John Rudge gave the visitors a
deserved lead with a glancing header past Alex Stepney. United struggled to find a breakthrough
but it seemed that fortune had smiled on them in the 65th minute when Frankie Prince was harshly
adjudged to have fouled winger Ian Storey-Moore in the penalty area. Justice was done, however,
when Dick Sheppard smothered George Best's penalty. Rovers now appeared to be coasting home,
but with 10 minutes remaining Charlton touched on Morgan's corner and substitute Sammy
McIlroy revived United's hopes with a headed goal. However, 4 minutes later Rovers regained their
lead, when Bruce Bannister left the United defence flat-footed to head home Stephens' corner and
Bristol Rovers had crowned one of their finest performances in the League Cup competition.

Rovers' exit in the next round was, therefore, a great anti-climax. Wolverhampton Wanderers'
4-0 win at Molineux was every bit as convincing as the scoreline suggests, and amply avenged the
2-0 triumph Rovers had notched against Wolves three months before in the Watney Cup.

All eyes on the ball as it flashes across the Wolves goal. The Rovers players pictured are John Rudge (third left) and Stuart Taylor (right).

A humiliating 1-0 away defeat by amateurs Hayes in the first round of the FA Cup was a blow to Eastville pride and manager Megson's attempts to attain a strong position in the League table were not helped by a series of injury problems. On 4 November, against Brentford at Eastville, Wayne Jones made what proved to be his final appearance for the club. A knee injury halted the career of this gifted midfield player, who only three days earlier had been named in Wales' sixteen-man squad for their crucial World Cup qualifying tie against England. He was only twenty-four years old. Barely two months later, goalkeeper Dick Sheppard suffered a depressed fracture of the skull making a typically plucky dive at Tranmere Rovers' Eddie Loyden's feet at Eastville and was sidelined for the rest of the season. Sheppard's mishap led to the signing, early in February, of twenty-six-year-old Jim Eadie from Cardiff City. The burly 6ft 2in Scot did not let in a single goal during his first five matches and Rovers soared up the table.

Manager Megson also created a new club record early in March when he signed centre forward Alan Warboys from Sheffield United for a £35,000 fee. Warboys and Megson had been playing colleagues at Sheffield Wednesday and during an interim stay with Cardiff City had proved a frequent scorer. He made his debut in the home match against Rochdale, partnering co-striker Bruce Bannister for the first time in a 0-0 draw. Promotion hopes began to flicker at Eastville again but they were effectively quashed in mid-March by two consecutive away defeats, 4-2 at Shrewsbury and 4-3 at Walsall. Rovers' young manager kept his players in the correct frame of mind, however, and a final sequence of four wins and a draw, helped by a late flourish of goals from Bannister and Warboys, boosted the goals total to seventy-seven (fifty-five of those at Eastville). This ensured qualification for the Watney Cup again as well as a respectable fifth position in the Third Division.

3

A SEASON TO REMEMBER

Don Megson had already been a major influence on the side as player-coach under Bill Dodgin's managership, inheriting a side which – as their two excursions into the Watney Cup clearly showed – had a tremendous ability to score goals, but it was the goals against column that most worried him. Megson, one of a new breed of shrewd post-war soccer managers, brought to Eastville the experience of more than 400 First Division games with Sheffield Wednesday, and a new sense of organisation. Whereas Rovers' football in the past had often been off-the-cuff, Megson brought a more scientific approach to their style, spending more time watching and analysing future opposition. There were things about the team the young manager inherited that were not characteristic of his ideas and preferences in football terms. He considered that promotion had been lost in the past because, 'although we have scored goals, we have given too many away'. His philosophy, at the beginning of 1973/74, was that there needed to be an extra man at the back, but with the full backs ready to overlap when the chance of the break comes. 'I find I have to field virtually two teams – one that is hard and tight in defence and another which can be attractive and creative in possession,' Megson stated. The wisdom of his thinking was clearly reflected in Rovers' performances, with fewer goals conceded than any other team in the Division during the promotion campaign.

Megson's first season as manager of Rovers was eventful to say the least, as it had started so stunningly with the Watney Cup triumph. However, it ended disappointingly with yet another near miss in the struggle for promotion, which was bound to create a sense of anti-climax. In 1972/73 Rovers lost only two League games at Eastville and scored more goals in front of their own fans than any other team in all four divisions. The previous season's away results cost the promotion which the home performances were good enough to earn. Cartilage trouble sidelined Mike Green for much of the season and this, combined with the injuries to Wayne Jones and Dick Sheppard, probably cost Rovers promotion. Chairman Douglas Mearns Milne bemoaned the great deal of bad luck that beset the team in the 1972/73 season. 'To lose one's goalkeeper and one of the key defensive men for a period covering the last third of the season is in itself difficult to overcome, but to be without the services of such a fine player as Wayne Jones from November, meant that the team was deprived of its "midfield-general" and one can not readily replace such talent from the club's own resources'.

It was a courageous step by Megson at the conclusion of his first year as team manager to transfer skipper Brian Godfrey and give free transfers to veterans Harold Jarman and Bobby Jones. Godfrey's ebullient midfield leadership made him a fans' favourite very soon after he arrived from Aston Villa, and Newport County paid £10,000 in June 1973 – a record for the Fourth Division club – for the thirty-three-year-old, who missed only four games in his first season and scored ten goals. Godfrey, who played for Everton, Scunthorpe United and Preston North End, joined Rovers in May 1971 from Aston Villa in the £48,000 exchange deal that took Ray Graydon to Villa Park. Jarman's popularity was a fact of Eastville life for more than a decade, and Jones' speed could always be relied upon to enliven most games. Yet, as one era ended, there was early evidence that the new one would be no less exciting than the old.

Through the course of the 1972/73 season, gradually rather than dramatically, a remoulding of the team took place. Only six members of the side that kicked off that season's League campaign played in the opening game at Bournemouth in August 1973: Bruce Bannister, Mike Green,

Lindsay Parsons, Tom Stanton, Kenny Stephens and Stuart Taylor. Mike Green was the new captain of the club following Godfrey's move to Newport County, and the only addition to the squad during the summer was the surprise signing of Trevor Jacobs from neighbours Bristol City, who had been all set to join Hereford United. The twenty-eight-year-old full-back, released by City, was signed to take over the No. 2 spot in Rovers' defence from Phil Roberts, as the Welsh Under-23 international had been sold to Portsmouth for £55,000. Plymouth Argyle, Newport County, Bury and Cardiff City were the teams, apart from Hereford, who had expressed an interest in Jacobs, who had made 145 first-team appearances for City, but Megson stepped in to sign the player whose defensive qualities and ball-winning ability he regarded highly.

The side assembled for the new season was built predominately from home-grown talent and free transfers. Jim Eadie, Trevor Jacobs, Mike Green, Kenny Stephens, Gordon Fearnley, Tom Stanton, Colin Dobson and Bryn Jones were all free transfers. John Rudge was valued at £5,000 when signed from Torquay United, but he was a straight swap for centre forward Robin Stubbs, so again Rovers did not have to pay out. Lindsay Parsons, Stuart Taylor, Frankie Prince, Peter Aitken and Jeff Coombes were home-grown players; Malcolm John was home-grown in that he started his career as an amateur in Rovers' youth team. But he was allowed to sign amateur forms for Swansea while at college in the Welsh city, and to sign him back as a professional after he had completed his studies, Rovers had to agree to pay a small sum for each of his first few senior matches. The major cost was the £58,000 Rovers paid for two forwards, Alan Warboys (£35,000) and Bruce Bannister (£23,000) and there can have been no more dynamic a duo at Rovers than the two Yorkshiremen. In 1972/73, the team's twin strikers, in the fifteen games after the partnership was first formed, scored twenty-one goals between them. Towards the end of the 1973/74 season Megson paid £20,000 for Dave Staniforth and obtained the services of Gerry O'Brien on a month's loan from First Division Southampton.

Bristol Rovers playing squad, 1973/74. From left to right, back row: Phil Bater, Geoff Williams, Jon Moore, Richard Crabtree, Peter Aitken, Wayne Powell, Kenny Stephens. Middle row: Bryn Jones, Tom Stanton, Mike Green, Stuart Taylor, Paul Lewis, Dick Sheppard, Jim Eadie, Alan Warboys, John Rudge, Frankie Prince, Lindsay Parsons. Front row: Bobby Campbell (trainer-coach), Trevor Jacobs, Malcolm John, Gordon Fearnley, Don Megson (manager) Bruce Bannister, David John, Martyn Britten, Colin Dobson (player-coach).

During the 1972/73 season the Football League announced that a three-up, three-down system would operate between the higher divisions from the following season, rather than the traditional two-up, two-down system. The four-up, four-down system between the Third and Fourth Divisions would continue, as would the re-election system between the League's bottom four clubs. At the time the four Football League divisions were designated First, Second, Third and Fourth, equivalent to the current Premier League, Championship, League One and League Two competitions. Until the 1975/76 season, clubs that finished level on points were separated by goal average; their total of goals for was divided by their goals against. This, it could be argued, encouraged defensive play, since not conceding any goals is obviously going to help the average. From 1976/77 onwards, goal difference was used instead, which is calculated by subtracting the goals against from the goals for. If clubs have the same goal difference, the one with most goals for is given the higher place.

Rovers made some improvements to the ground during the close season, with new turnstile arrangements allowing direct entry into the North Enclosure and North Stand, and additional entrances at the Muller Road End, together with improved floodlighting and a bigger and better match-day programme (price 10p). In October 1973 it was thought that Eastville Stadium was the only football ground in the League that did not display commercial advertisements, but following negotiations between Rovers and the Greyhound Co. that changed.

As the 1973/74 season kicked off Rovers celebrated their ninetieth anniversary with a number of changes, reverting to the popular blue-and-white-quartered shirts being the most visible. In 1962, the last season that the famous blue-and-white quarters were worn, Rovers had slumped back into the Third Division and in the changes that swept through the club that following summer, the distinctive strip became one of the scapegoats. Considered by some as a desire to go back, Club Secretary Peter Terry commented, 'The strip may incorporate a traditional design, but it's modern-looking,' and somewhat prophetically, he 'hoped these things would help make season 1973/74 a season to remember'.

Rovers had embarked on a short pre-season tour of Rhodesia, winning their first match 2-1 against Salisbury. The party, including manager Don Megson and coach Colin Dobson, also ran

a series of coaching demonstrations for schools before travelling on to Victoria Falls. The pre-season friendly against Newport County at Somerton Park on 3 August quickly reunited former Rovers' captain Brian Godrey and Eastville idol Harold Jarman with their ex-teammates. Megson's line-up, giving an indication of his plans for the coming season, included, as captain, Mike Green who had made only one first-team appearance since November 1972, the twenty-six-year-old defender having suffered a series of fitness setbacks after undergoing a knee operation the following February. Colin Dobson, who spent the final three months of the previous season on the injured list with foot trouble, also made his comeback in the friendly match, with new signing Trevor Jacobs taking over at right-back from Phil Roberts. Rovers, in their only warm-up game before defending the

Captain Mike Green leads out the team at Eastville at the beginning of the season.

Watney Cup the following Saturday, soon took the lead in the 11th minute with a neatly headed goal by John Rudge from Dobson's flighted free-kick following a foul by Coldrick on Warboys. Bruce Bannister played a major part in Rovers' second goal 7 minutes later, beating three defenders in the course of a 35yd run before accurately crossing the ball for Warboys, who had time to pick his spot before hammering it past Macey in Newport's goal. However, a couple of minutes later, Newport's captain Brian Harris sent a long ball across the field to an unmarked Harold Jarman, who slammed the ball into the roof of the net from close range. Dick Sheppard, who had his skull fractured in January 1972, came on as Rovers' substitute goalkeeper for the second half, and within minutes was beaten twice by shots from his old teammate Brian Godfrey, but on both occasions the ball crashed against the post. Substitute Rod Jones scored a deserved equaliser for Newport from another accurate Harris pass in the last minute while Rovers stood appealing for offside.

A Match-by-Match Record of Bristol Rovers' Results during the 1973/74 Season

SATURDAY 11 AUGUST 1973, EASTVILLE STADIUM WATNEY CUP 1ST ROUND

Bristol Rovers 1 – Bannister
West Ham United 1 – MacDougall
Half-time: 1-1
Attendance: 19,974
Referee: Bill Gow (Swansea)

Rovers won 5-4 on penalties. Rovers' scorers: Dobson, Warboys, Prince, Green, Bannister. West Ham scorers: Taylor, Brooking, Bonds, MacDougall.

Bristol Rovers: Eadie, Jacobs, Parsons, Green, Taylor, Prince, Stephens, Rudge, Warboys, Bannister, Dobson. Substitute: Fearnley for Rudge (57 mins)

West Ham United: Ferguson, McDowell, Lampard, Bonds, Taylor, Moore, Ayris, Holland, MacDougall, Brooking, Robson. Substitutes: Tyler for Ayris (60 mins), Lock for McDowell (68 mins)

Don Megson was not best pleased over the caution Frankie Prince picked up in the Gloucestershire FA Professional Cup Final at the end of the previous season. The booking against City took Prince over the twelve-point penalty limit and brought him a two-match suspension. But the ban did not include Watney Cup matches, so Prince was eligible to face West Ham, but could not play in the next two testing away matches at Bournemouth. West Ham's objectives for their visit to Eastville were to end their dismal record against minnows in cup competitions, and to ensure two more competitive matches before the start of the season. The cultured Londoners, including stars like Ted MacDougall, Bryan Robson, the First Division's leading scorer the previous season, and England

Match ticket for the pre-season Watney Cup tie against West Ham United.

Mike Green, Frankie Prince and Stuart Taylor are unable to prevent West Ham forward Ted MacDougall getting a shot in during the Watney Cup tie.

captain Bobby Moore, had one of their strongest and best balanced squads in years available to manager Ron Greenwood. Rovers set up their first attack from the kick-off, when Prince sent Rudge away, and after an interchange of passes Bannister was able to get in a shot, but it lacked power. Immediately afterwards Bannister found himself clear in the box but was tackled and the ball lobbed harmlessly over the bar. West Ham came into the game for the first time when Bobby Moore's shrewd pass put Trevor Brooking through but Mike Green intercepted quickly. Again Moore brought danger with a floated free-kick, but this time Trevor Jacobs, in his first competitive game for Rovers, coolly intercepted and cleared the ball. Rovers came closest to scoring when Rudge shot just over the bar from 20yds, and another chance came when Bannister shot hard and accurately, but the ball was charged down for a corner by Lampard. After 25 minutes, from a free-kick taken by Moore, West Ham had their first clear-cut chance to score when Ted MacDougall pushed the ball across the face of the goal to Bonds, but the ball was scrambled away. On the half-hour Rovers went ahead thanks to a fine piece of opportunism by debutant Jacobs. Pat Holland tried to keep the ball in play just inside the halfway line, but Jacobs nipped in, beat Tommy Taylor, and crossed to the far post. There Warboys rose to head back to the effervescent Bannister, who nodded the ball past Ferguson. Seven minutes later a cross by Holland was harmlessly gathered by Stuart Taylor, but then he and Prince seemed undecided about what to do with the ball and MacDougall nipped in to slide the ball into the net at the near post.

West Ham looked more determined in attack after the interval with a Brooking shot bringing a diving clearance from Eadie, followed by a swerving lef-foot shot which was safely gathered by the goalkeeper. Rovers' first second-half attempt was by Bannister, but his shot went straight at Ferguson, then Stephens had a much better chance, but he took too long and the ball was cleared. After 69 minutes Bannister set up a good chance with a back-heel to Warboys, who hit the ball straight at Ferguson, and a couple of minutes later Rovers had an opportunity to go ahead when Ferguson mishandled a high cross from Jacobs, but Warboys, facing the wrong way, lobbed it over the bar. In the closing seconds, Fearnley was desperately unlucky when the ball came out from the underside of the crossbar, and with the teams still level after 90 minutes the tie went to a sudden-death penalty decider. Incredibly, goal-poacher Bryan Robson twice failed to score with West Ham's first spot kick. Jim Eadie saved the first kick, but the linesman indicated that the Rovers goalkeeper had moved, and when the kick was taken again Eadie guessed correctly and made a fine save, just inside the post. Colin Dobson stepped up first for Rovers to score past

Jim Eadie dives to save the first of two penalties taken by West Ham's Bryan Robson. A minute later Eadie made his second save – and the Hammers were on their way out of the Watney Cup.

Bobby Ferguson, the rest of the penalties being a formality with Bannister netting the fifth and winning spot kick for Rovers. So Rovers began their defence of the Watney Cup where they had left off in winning it the previous season – by banging in the penalties.

TUESDAY 14 AUGUST 1973, EASTVILLE STADIUM   WATNEY CUP SEMI-FINAL

Bristol Rovers	0
Hull City	1 – Lord
Half-time:	0-0
Attendance:	12,693
Referee:	Gordon Kew (Amersham)
Bristol Rovers:	Eadie, Jacobs, Parsons, Green, Taylor, Prince, Stephens, Fearnley, Warboys, Bannister, Dobson. Substitutes: Stanton for Prince (74 mins), Bryn Jones for Stephens (74 mins)
Hull City:	Wealands, Banks, De Vries, Galvin, Deere, Kaye, Lord, McGill, Pearson, Wagstaff, Greenwood. Substitute: Hemmerman.

Rovers, attempting to be the first club to retain the Watney Cup, were without striker John Rudge, who had failed a late fitness test and was replaced by Gordon Fearnley for the money-spinning semi-final against a Hull side managed by former Arsenal and Northern Ireland international Terry Neill. Rovers' boss Don Megson reminded his players that although they had beaten West Ham

Alan Warboys, Gordon Fearnley and Bruce Bannister put pressure on the Hull City defence during the Watney Cup semi-final.

and were facing a side from a lower division than the Hammers, Rovers were still the underdogs. The Rovers chief had received reports on Saturday's match in which Hull trounced Mansfield Town 3-0, and considered the danger men to be long-serving Ken Wagstaff, last season's top scorer Stuart Pearson, and new signing Chris Galvin from Leeds United. Rovers' chances of winning the game really came in the first half when Colin Dobson crashed a shot over the bar, Kenny Stephens brought a diving save from Jeff Wealands and Frankie Prince hit a shot which bounced out of the goalkeeper's arms but which he managed to grab at the second attempt. Had Rovers scored in the first half-hour when they really put Hull under pressure then the outcome might well have been different, but Hull gradually wore down the Rovers enthusiasm and gained control of midfield.

The only goal came after 55 minutes when referee Gordon Kew overruled a linesman's flag for offside as Hull attacked. The ball ran to Chris Galvin who hit a weak shot at goal which went wide, but the referee spotted a deflection by a Rovers defender and awarded a corner. From Roy Greenwood's cross Malcolm Lord dashed in to head inside a strangely unguarded near post. Rovers continued to fight for every ball, and with 16 minutes remaining manager Don Megson courageously made a double substitution, replacing midfield men Frankie Prince and Kenny Stephens with Bryn Jones and Tom Stanton. Rovers gathered themselves for a final onslaught and might have had a penalty when Gordon Fearnley's shot appeared to be blocked by a defender's hand, but the referee dismissed the appeals and waved play on. They then once more achieved the nearest of misses when a Fearnley header from a corner was trapped by Jeff Wealands between his legs, resulting in a tremendous melee in the goalmouth – but no goal. So the holders of the cup went out of the competition and hopes of a money-spinning all-Bristol Watney Cup final between Rovers and City were dashed when the two clubs lost their respective semi-finals against Hull City and Stoke City. However, Rovers did make a five-figure profit from the competition as Watneys gave them £4,000 for qualifying and £500 for winning their first-round tie. They also received approximately £2,000 in television fees and approximately £4,000 from their share of the net gate receipts.

On Saturday 18 August, the day when Rovers would have preferred to have been attempting to retain the Watney Cup, they travelled to Home Park for a friendly match with Plymouth Argyle. Colin Dobson took charge of the injury-hit team as manager Don Megson watched Bournemouth – Rovers' opponents in the first League game of the season – win 1-0 at West Bromwich Albion. Without Warboys, Rudge and Dobson, who were injured, and Prince, who was suspended, the main aim of the game was to give a run to some of the players who did not appear in the Watney Cup ties.

The Rovers team was: Eadie, Jacobs, Parsons, Green, Taylor, Stanton, Jones (B), Bannister, Fearnley, John (M), Aitken. The substitutes were: Powell, Stephens and Crabtree. The 2,383 crowd saw a below-par Rovers performance; lacking power up front they rarely threatened Jim Furnell in the Plymouth goal. Young Richard Crabtree took over in goal from Jim Eadie at half-time, but was beaten by Hinch after 58 minutes, when he rounded the goalkeeper to score, and a Dave Provan penalty after 65 minutes, after Jacobs had brought down veteran winger Harry Burrows. Without Warboys and Rudge, Rovers had little to offer up front, but when they did get the chance to pull one back in the closing minutes, Gordon Fearnley's shot rebounded to safety off Wayne Powell. Rovers finished the game with ten men when Peter Aitken went off with a slight strain after all three substitutes had been brought on. Argyle manager Tony Waiters commented, 'I can't see Rovers playing like that when the season starts next Saturday'. How right he was!

SATURDAY 25 AUGUST 1973, DEAN COURT, BOSCOMBE

Bournemouth	0
Bristol Rovers	3 – Warboys (2), Bannister
Half-time:	0-0
Attendance:	11,379
Referee:	Ken Baker (Rugby)
Bournemouth:	Baker, Howe, Miller, Benson, Delaney, Powell, Gabriel, Boyer, Clark, Cave, Groves. Substitute: De Garis
Bristol Rovers:	Eadie, Jacobs, Parsons, Green, Taylor, Stanton, Stephens, Jones (B), Warboys, Bannister, Dobson.
	Substitute: Fearnley for Stephens (half-time)

Kenny Stephens sends over a cross to the advancing Alan Warboys in the 3-0 victory over Bournemouth.

Alan Warboys beats two Bournemouth defenders, Delaney and Benson, during the opening League fixture at Dean Court.

Don Megson decided on a 4-4-2 formation for the opening League game against Bournemouth, considered to be promotion rivals at the start of the season by the Rovers manager. Watched by a large contingent of Bristol fans taking advantage of the Bank Holiday weekend, Rovers attacked directly into the brilliant sun in the first half of the game, played in sweltering heat. Rovers, after absorbing first-half pressure from Bournemouth, who often moved with promise from midfield but failed to penetrate Rovers' back four, gradually began to take command. Rovers were denied a 35th-minute goal by a brilliant save from Kieron Baker, who sprang to his right to hold a 25yd Bryn Jones volley that looked certain to end up in the net. Kenny Stephens had a chip cleared off the line by Delaney, with the home goalkeeper stranded, and from the resulting corner Stuart Taylor shot over the bar.

Five minutes from half-time Stephens was carried off for attention, returning a few minutes later with his left ankle strapped, but was replaced by Gordon Fearnley after half-time. Two minutes after the break, Jacobs became the second Rovers player to be booked for a second foul in quick succession on winger Alan Groves. Lindsay Parsons had picked up his second booking of the season with the game 11 minutes old when he brought down former Bristol City forward Brian Clark. Following an incredible escape when Groves slammed a shot onto the inside of the post, the ball ricocheting across the goal line to safety, Rovers took the lead with a 55th-minute goal from Warboys. Jones won the ball from Bristolian Tony Powell just inside Bournemouth's half and advanced before slipping forward a pass which Warboys hammered into the top near corner of the goal. Rovers scored again in the 70th minute with another great goal for Warboys, who turned on a Bannister pass to beat Baker with a fierce shot that entered the net off the inside of the far post. Ten minutes from the end Bannister nipped in to head in from Dobson's corner from the left.

Rovers' formation had worked well for them, succeeding in tying up Bournemouth in midfield and shutting out their attack, so much so that manger John Bond lambasted his side's opening day performance as 'disgraceful'. Rovers, on the other hand, were off to a great start.

WEDNESDAY 29 AUGUST 1973, DEAN COURT, BOSCOMBE   LEAGUE CUP 1ST ROUND

Bournemouth	1 – Redknapp
Bristol Rovers	0
Half-time:	0-0
Attendance:	7,530
Referee:	Jim Bent (Hemel Hempstead)
Bournemouth:	Baker, Machin, Howe, Benson, Delaney, Gabriel, Redknapp, Feely, Cave, Powell, Buttle. Substitute: De Garis for Delaney (58 mins)
Bristol Rovers:	Eadie, Jacobs, Parsons, Green, Taylor, Stanton, Fearnley, Jones (B), Warboys, Bannister, Dobson. Substitute: John (M)

Bournemouth, severely shaken by the home League defeat on Saturday, reshuffled their team for the first-round League Cup tie on the Wednesday evening. Striker Brian Clark and winger Alan Groves were axed, with Phil Boyer ruled out with a leg injury. Steve Buttle, the midfield player signed from Ipswich Town, came in for his debut and ex-West Ham winger Harry Redknapp and former Chelsea striker Peter Feely were brought in to the attack. Rovers started with the same side that had ended the League fixture, but there was to be no repeat of the dominance displayed by Rovers five days earlier. However, in the first half there was a suggestion that it might happen as Bournemouth nervously closed their ranks – just as if they were the visiting team – but gradually they began to look more like a side geared to make an impact on the Third Division.

There were two main reasons for the transformation. Firstly, the conditions; Saturday's firm, true pitch had acquired a slippery surface that prevented Rovers achieving the same high degree of accuracy and control that Bournemouth had found so devastating. Secondly, Bournemouth bolstered their defence with an extra man in the back line. Rovers had their chances early on when a mistake by Jimmy Gabriel let in Fearnley, and a prolific drive by Warboys was deflected high over the bar. Goalkeeper Kieron Baker made a couple of saves on the line in as many minutes, and held a low drive from Colin Dobson, who cut inside following a fine run by Bruce Bannister. Centre half John Delaney stuck his foot out in the nick of time when Warboys appeared a certain scorer just on the half-hour. Steve Buttle headed home for Bournemouth but had the 'goal' struck off for offside. Just before the hour, manager John Bond took off Delaney and sent on midfielder Jimmy de Garis, which brought a quick reward as within 4 minutes Bournemouth had scored their winning goal. Jimmy Gabriel's penetrating run down the right resulted in a low cross that was only partially cleared. Harry Redknapp snapped up the ball and played a pass to Micky Cave, who headed the ball back down into the winger's path for him to guide a shot past the out-rushing Jim Eadie. So there was to be no League Cup thrills at Eastville this season after three years in the limelight.

SATURDAY 1 SEPTEMBER 1973, EASTVILLE STADIUM

Bristol Rovers	2 – Warboys, Bannister
Charlton Athletic	1 – Horsfield
Half-time:	1-1
Attendance:	7,323
Referee:	Bert Newsome (Shropshire)
Bristol Rovers:	Eadie, Jacobs, Parsons, Green, Taylor, Prince, Jones (B), Stanton, Warboys, Bannister, Dobson. Substitute: Fearnley
Charlton Athletic:	Forster, Jones (M), Tumbridge, Smart, Shipperley, Curtis, Powell, Davies, Peacock, Horsfield, Flanagan. Substitute: Arnold for Tumbridge (80 mins)

Tom Stanton and Colin Dobson
congratulate Alan Warboys
on scoring Rovers' equalising
goal against Charlton Athletic.

The joint efforts of Charlton's
Tumbridge and goalkeeper
Forster can't stop Bannister
scoring Rovers' second goal –
his 100th League goal.

Playing towards the Tote End in the first half, Rovers did all the attacking in the early stages of Eastville's opening League match of the season, but slipped behind after 18 minutes to a goal by former Swindon Town striker Arthur Horsfield. After linking up with his ex-Swindon teammate Roger Smart, Horsfield hammered in a close-range shot which goalkeeper Jim Eadie got a hand to but couldn't prevent flying into the roof of the net. Charlton may well have added a quick second had it not been for a timely challenge by Frankie Prince to deflect a Flanagan shot following a good pass by Peacock. Rovers regained their confidence and almost snatched an equaliser when a Dobson free-kick was flicked on by Bannister to Warboys who, lunging forward, just failed to make contact with the ball. Ten minutes before half-time Rovers were level following a fine move, instigated by Stanton who beat two men and pushed a pass to Mike Green on the right. His centre was met with a full length diving header by Stuart Taylor who sent the ball cannoning onto the inside of the far post. As it rebounded across the goal line the ball was stabbed in by Warboys.

Only 4 minutes after the restart Rovers took the lead. Tom Stanton, tireless in midfield throughout the game, just failed to make contact with a Bryn Jones centre from the right, the ball carrying on across to Dobson on the left. He promptly knocked the ball back into the goalmouth to

Warboys whose shot was blocked by Tumbridge, and as the defence struggled to get the ball away Bruce Bannister nipped in to force the ball over the line. It was the Yorkshireman's 100th League goal, and he nearly added to his tally when a poor backpass from Forster was chased by Bannister, needing a frantic lunging dive by the goalkeeper to snatch the ball from just in front of the speedy Rovers' striker.

Six minutes from the end Eadie was unable to hold Peacock's shot and the ball rebounded off his chest to Powell, who fired onto a post and the ball was scrambled away. It was enough to stir Rovers into a spell of furious activity, and in the closing stages Bannister and Warboys had goalbound shots blocked and Smart headed a drive from Frankie Prince off the line with Forster beaten. Despite the victory, manager Megson's feelings were that Rovers had 'played poorly by our own standards', with the wet conditions a contributing factor.

SATURDAY 8 SEPTEMBER 1973, BLUNDELL PARK, CLEETHORPES

Grimsby Town	1 – Chatterley (penalty)
Bristol Rovers	1 – Jones
Half-time:	1-1
Attendance:	7,640
Referee:	Alan Porter (Bolton)
Grimsby Town:	Wainman, Beardsley, Booth, Chatterley, Wigginton, Gray, Brace, Barton, Hubbard, Hickman, Sharp. Substitute: Boylen for Sharp (76 mins)
Bristol Rovers:	Eadie, Jacobs, Parsons, Green, Taylor, Prince, Jones (B), Stanton, Warboys, Bannister, Dobson. Substitute: Stephens

Facing a Grimsby side seeking their first point of the season, Megson named an unchanged side despite having not played particularly well against Charlton, with new Grimsby boss Ron Ashman fielding the line-up that had lost 1-0 at Chesterfield. On a misty afternoon, Rovers were quick to put the home side under pressure with an attack led by Dobson down the left, followed by a long shot from Prince that went over the bar, and home 'keeper Wainman had to move smartly across his line to prevent an own goal from a back header by Beardsley. Megson's decision to give Bryn Jones another chance in the side reaped a quick reward when he gave Rovers an 11th-minute lead. Warboys pushed a pass to Bannister, who whipped the ball through to put Jones clear, scoring his first goal of the season with an angled shot which Wainman got his hands to but was unable to hold. Rovers hunted for a second goal with Warboys volleying wide when he might have scored, and Jones, encouraged by his goal, beat three defenders in a weaving run before turning the ball to Bannister, whose quick shot was deflected for a corner by Gray.

Bruce Bannister heads for the Grimsby goal with Tom Stanton in support.

Grimsby began to come into the game more, firstly with a lob from right-back Beardsley that dropped just behind the bar, and then a cross from the right by Hubbard gave Eadie trouble, the Rovers goalkeeper pushing the ball out to Sharp, but the winger shot into the side netting. Grimsby equalised after 33 minutes from a penalty following an inexplicable hand-ball by Mike Green. As Wigginton sent a long free-kick, dropping into Rovers' penalty area, Green needlessly palmed the ball down. Chatterley took the kick, hitting it hard and low to the right of the diving Eadie. Rovers had the chance to score again in the early stages of the second half when Dobson squared the ball to Prince, who was just wide with a first-time shot. Rovers continued to produce the more impressive football; their 4-4-2 formation, with the midfield men sweeping forward and back in attack, held mastery for long periods, bringing a string of saves from Wainman, one a leaping save from Dobson's free-kick, awarded for a foul on Bannister. However, in the dying seconds, Rovers were almost beaten by a long shot from Chatterley, but Eadie saved brilliantly, pushing the ball over the bar. Warboys and Bannister proved themselves a formidable duo up front, whilst in defence Taylor looked safe enough, Parsons played well and Prince's efforts kept the backline tight. Jones had a vastly improved game, Stanton worked tirelessly in midfield and Dobson's skill kept up a good service to the strikers.

TUESDAY 11 SEPTEMBER 1973, EASTVILLE STADIUM

Bristol Rovers	1 – Taylor
Hereford United	1 – Redrobe
Half-time:	0-1
Attendance:	12,620
Referee:	Clive White (Harrow)
Bristol Rovers:	Eadie, Jacobs, Parsons, Green, Taylor, Prince, Stephens, Stanton, Warboys, Bannister, Dobson. Substitute: Fearnley for Stephens (82 mins)
Hereford United:	Hughes, Carver, Naylor, McLaughlin, Tucker, Tavener, Evans, Jenkins, Redrobe, Gregory, Mallender. Substitute: Owen for Jenkins (75 mins)

It was Hereford's debut visit to Eastville for a League match, having been runners-up in the Fourth Division in 1972/73 in their first season in the Football League. Manager Colin Addison had a setback at the start of the season when goalkeeper David Icke was forced to give up the game, at the age of twenty-one, with an arthritic condition. Fred Potter, hero of the club's famous FA Cup run in the 1971/72 season, was recalled to the side but broke his wrist in the opening game. This prompted Addison to sign the former Chelsea 'keeper Tommy Hughes from Aston Villa. Rovers' new floodlights were switched on for the first time in a League match, the lights boosted to colour-television-standard specifications by Colston Electrical Co. at a cost of £10,000. However, the new lights did nothing to illuminate the home side's play as Hughes, in Hereford's goal, went in for the break untested, whereas Jim Eadie was beaten in the 7th minute from the first corner of the game. Striker Eric Redrobe met Brian Evans' left wing corner at the near post and nodded the ball down through a crowd of players into the far corner of the net.

Rovers' strikers had difficulty in finding a way through a resolute Hereford defence, not helped by many of Rovers' passes going astray and their flair players Stephens and Dobson unable to impose their skills on the game. Just before the hour, Tommy Hughes, who had been a bystander, became Hereford's hero of the night. First he did well to save a 30yd free-kick from Tom Stanton and Rovers, striving for an equaliser, broke away on the right and McLaughlin fouled Bruce Bannister in the penalty area. However, the goalkeeper hurled himself at Bannister's fierce spot kick to beat the ball away for a corner. Rovers' bid to save the game should have been quashed with 9 minutes remaining when Stuart Taylor felled Redrobe with a clumsy challenge, but Redrobe himself struck the spot kick wide of goal. Taylor then saved Rovers' unbeaten record with a dramatic injury time equaliser. Colin Dobson's flighted free-kick to the far post was nodded goalwards by Warboys, only to be headed out by Ken Mallender from under the bar, but Taylor was there to head the ball home. The ball crossed the line before it was scrambled away for substitute Gordon Fearnley to ram it back into the goal, to the delight of the relieved Rovers fans.

Hereford's Tommy Hughes is beaten by a header from Alan Warboys, but Ken Mallender heads off the line.

Stuart Taylor (No. 5) towers above Bruce Bannister to head in Rovers' late equalising goal against Hereford United.

SATURDAY 15 SEPTEMBER 1973, EASTVILLE STADIUM

Bristol Rovers	2 – Stanton (2)
Halifax Town	0
Half-time:	1-0
Attendance:	7,485
Referee:	Alan Turvey (Wickford)
Bristol Rovers:	Eadie, Jacobs, Parsons, Green, Taylor, Prince, Stephens, Stanton, Warboys, Bannister, Dobson. Substitute: Fearnley
Halifax Town:	Smith, Burgin, Quinn, Pugh, Pickering, Rhodes, Jones, Wilkie, Ford, Gwyther, Hale. Substitute: Shanahan for Wilkie (70 mins)

Halifax visited Eastville in a mid-table position having drawn three of their first four games and suffering a 4-1 trouncing by Grimsby in the other. Lindsay Parsons came through a late fitness test to preserve his three-year appearance record of 172 first-team games and Rovers fielded an unchanged side. Halifax included John Quinn, who had played alongside Don Megson in the 1966 Sheffield Wednesday FA Cup final line-up. The morning's heavy rain had softened the pitch considerably but conditions were good as Rovers, with an unbeaten League record to preserve, kicked towards the Muller Road End in the first half. Halifax quickly settled into a defensive formation with Hale sweeping up behind the back four, but it was the Yorkshire club who first threatened as Prince stroked an ill-judged backpass to Eadie, which Whittle moved on to swiftly. Green came to Rovers' rescue with a challenge that brought Halifax a corner. Rovers retaliated with an attack down the left by Dobson, but his chip into the goalmouth was plucked off Warboys' head by Alex Smith. Halifax had a couple of chances that were dealt with comfortably by Eadie, while Rovers were denied by Ken Hale, who made a goal-line clearance from Warboys. Kenny Stephens prised an opening, and as his shot was beaten out by goalkeeper Smith, the Rovers right-winger hit the ball back into the crowded goalmouth. Warboys helped the drive on, but with Smith grounded Hale scooped the ball around for a corner. Three minutes before half-time, Rovers eventually went ahead with the first goal of the season for Tom Stanton. Prince hit a pass to Dobson and as the ball was chipped into Halifax's penalty area, Stanton raced through to force the ball past Smith.

Rovers should have increased their lead 8 minutes after the restart when Prince missed a good chance, mistiming his shot. Rovers' defence was badly exposed midway through the second half when Ford, taking a pass from Quinn on the left, drove over a low centre which sped across the goalmouth and past the far post for a goal kick. Gwyther wasted a good chance of equalising for the visitors when he shot tamely at Eadie after a Burgin pass was helped on to him by Ford.

With 11 minutes remaining Stanton moved up to hammer in his second goal of the game when the ball came loose, following an attack led by Dobson and Bannister which had been partially foiled. It was the first time in six years of League football that the Scot had scored twice in one game. Seconds from the end, Warboys almost added a third when he sent a diving header inches wide.

Tom Stanton slips through the Halifax Town defence to shoot in the first of his two goals in a 2-0 win.

Colin Dobson, watched by Bannister, is tackled to prevent another goalscoring chance against Halifax.

Despite a laborious performance against poor opposition, Rovers' two points lifted them into second place in the table.

TUESDAY 18 SEPTEMBER 1973, GAY MEADOW, SHREWSBURY

Shrewsbury Town	0
Bristol Rovers	2 – Prince, King (own goal)
Half-time:	0-2
Attendance:	3,015
Referee:	Edward Jolly (Manchester)
Shrewsbury Town:	Mulhearn, King, Calloway, Matthias, Kemp, Durban, Roberts (D), Moir, Kearney, Tarbuck, Butler. Substitute: Roberts (I) for Moir (77 mins)
Bristol Rovers:	Eadie, Jacobs, Parsons, Green, Taylor, Prince, Stephens, Stanton, Warboys, Bannister, Dobson. Substitute: Fearnley

The trip to Gay Meadow saw Rovers hit peak form, easily sweeping aside bottom-of-the-table Shrewsbury to go top of the Third Division table. Rovers, enjoying more freedom of movement than they had been allowed in home games, were yards faster than the home side and stroked the ball around delightfully, taking the lead after 18 minutes when Frankie Prince, backing up the attack in the way Tom Stanton did so effectively against Halifax, took advantage of the attention Warboys was attracting. Warboys sliced his shot across the penalty area and the ball ran straight to Prince, who was standing all on his own 12yds from the goal, from where he calmly picked his spot in the left-hand corner of the net. Rovers had full control of the midfield and were much quicker to the ball and it was no surprise when they scored a second goal on the stroke of half-time. Colin Dobson and Bruce Bannister set the ball up for Warboys, who flicked it on to Kenny Stephens. The Rovers winger, coming in from the right, let fly with a terrific, angled first-time shot, which full-back John King deflected into the net between 'keeper Ken Mulhearn and the near post.

It was not quite so comfortable for Rovers in the second-half and Town's new signing Alan Durban, the former Derby County and Welsh international, brought a great diving save from Eadie. The new Shrewsbury captain then hit the side netting with a strong shot and Laurie Calloway brought another save from Eadie. Rovers lost a little of their first-half dominance but Taylor and Green were superb in repelling Shrewsbury's new found confidence. The only black mark in an impressive Rovers display came when Bruce Bannister was booked late in the second half for arguing with the referee. The decisive victory illustrated two points: firstly, Rovers, despite the evidence of the first three home games, were still an exciting team to watch; and secondly, they were far from being a two-man team, as their early dependence on Bruce Bannister and Alan Warboys had suggested.

SATURDAY 22 SEPTEMBER 1973, EWOOD PARK, BLACKBURN

Blackburn Rovers	0
Bristol Rovers	2 – Bannister, Warboys
Half-time:	0-1
Attendance:	8,424
Referee:	Michael Lowe (Sheffield)
Blackburn Rovers:	Jones, Wilkinson, Arentoft, Garbett, Martin, Fazackerley, Field, Metcalfe, Napier, Parkes, Hutchins. Substitute: Endean for Hutchins (half-time)
Bristol Rovers:	Eadie, Jacobs, Parsons, Green, Taylor, Prince, Stephens, Stanton, Warboys, Bannister, Dobson. Substitute: Fearnley for Stephens (75 mins)

Don Megson's team travelled to Lancashire as joint leaders of the Third Division with Tranmere Rovers. With an unbeaten record, having taken ten points from a possible twelve, they had to face a talented Blackburn side with a 100 per cent home record. The Pirates made their customary guarded start, allowing Blackburn to take the initiative early on, although the only time the Rovers goal looked in danger Eadie saved from Field without much difficulty. Rovers began to break out and a long cross into the goalmouth by Jacobs was touched out from above Warboys' head, and a first-time shot from Prince was saved low down by Jones. Dobson, looking sharp on the left, slipped through a telling pass for Bannister to take in his stride, but a quick-covering Martin blocked

Bruce Bannister ends a four-match spell without a goal by putting Rovers into the lead at Blackburn.

the striker's low shot. Rovers again moved on the attack with Stanton flicking the ball to find Bannister unmarked and with Roger Jones well out from his line, Bannister scored with a skilfully judged lob over the goalkeeper. The opportunist 17th-minute goal was the striker's first goal in five games.

Rovers went close to adding a second when Stanton brought a good save from Jones with a powerful drive. Stanton, powerful and energetic in midfield, then sent Stephens away down the right but his centre was plucked off Bannister's head by the 'keeper. Another foray on the right wing by Jacobs brought a similar centre and a similar save – this time to foil Warboys. Blackburn brought on Barry Endean for the start of the second half, which began in heavy rain, and looked considerably sharper. Field moved in from the left and Parkes ran across his teammate to take the strike and with Eadie beaten, it fell to Lindsay Parsons to whip the ball away from inside the far post. Napier was felled by Taylor's tackle on the edge of the penalty area but the referee refused to give a free-kick. Rovers seemed to have weathered the storm and began to put Blackburn under pressure again, creating chances for Bannister, Prince and Stephens. Four minutes from the end Rovers scored a second goal when substitute Gordon Fearnley, on for Kenny Stephens, sent a perfect through pass to Warboys who scored from close range. By an adjustment of tactics, Rovers, whose away form was so dismal the previous season, had made themselves the most feared visitors in the division. The two-point haul at Ewood Park opened up a clear lead at the top of the Third Division as Tranmere were beaten 2-1 at Bournemouth.

SATURDAY 29 SEPTEMBER 1973, EASTVILLE STADIUM

Bristol Rovers	1 – Dobson
Cambridge United	0
Half-time:	0-0
Attendance:	9,189
Referee:	Alan Robinson (Portsmouth)
Bristol Rovers:	Eadie, Jacobs, Parsons, Green, Taylor, Prince, Stephens, Stanton, Warboys, Bannister, Dobson. Substitute: Fearnley
Cambridge United:	Vasper, Harris, Akers, Eades, Rathbone, Watson, Ferguson, Greenhalgh, Lill, Guild, Leonard. Substitute: Ross

Cambridge United, in their first-ever season in Division Three, had yet to take a point away from home, although success on their own ground had given them a respectable League placing. Manager Bill Lievers recalled the powerful Alan Guild as an extra defender in a bid to pick up their first away point of the season. Cambridge faced a bright sun as they kicked towards the Tote End in the first half, but it was Rovers who were the first to threaten as Warboys sent a powerful header just over the bar from a Stephens corner. It was quickly followed by a Prince cross from the left that caused danger, and then another Rovers advance down the left by Bannister brought a hurried clearance by Akers, who was happy to concede a corner as Stephens raced in at the far post. Mike Green out-jumped the Cambridge defence to meet Stephens' resulting corner, but Vasper saved.

Taylor was penalised for a foul on Lill 10yds outside the area, but Ferguson's attempt at goal sailed a yard over the bar. Rovers continued to look threatening and were unlucky not to take the lead after 28 minutes when Dobson, in lively form on the left, hammered a 30yd shot onto the Cambridge crossbar. The rebound was scrambled away by Akers only for Stephens to pump the ball back into the goalmouth, where Bannister turned a pass into Prince's path, but the midfield man's shot went wide. Rovers immediately went back on the attack at the start of the second half and forced a corner on the left, but when Warboys climbed high to meet Dobson's kick Akers blocked the ball on the goal line. Then Dobson, displaying his wide variety of skills, clipped over a perfect centre which Warboys headed just wide. The breakthrough Rovers deserved came after 65 minutes with a goal scored by player-coach Colin Dobson. Bannister won the ball out on Rovers' right and crossed it to Prince, who lobbed the ball on to Dobson, who scored his first goal of the season with a brilliant volley, hooking the ball as he fell out of the reach of Vasper.

It was the goal Rovers needed to draw Cambridge out of what had been a frustratingly effective defensive shell. Rovers went close again when Vasper could only parry a powerful Stephens shot,

Clever ball control in the penalty area by Bannister is watched by Warboys and a ring of Cambridge defenders.

The only goal of the game against Cambridge United, hooked in by Colin Dobson past Allan Harris.

which Bannister followed up quickly with a second attempt that the goalkeeper got his body behind. Bannister also had a late header bounce on top of the bar and over. Although they only had one goal to show for their superiority, the game showed that Rovers could overcome the problem presented by ultra-defensive formations.

29 SEPTEMBER 1973

	P	W	D	L	F	A	Pts
ROVERS	8	6	2	0	14	3	14
Oldham Athletic	8	4	4	0	8	3	12
York City	8	4	3	1	15	11	11
Tranmere Rovers	8	4	2	2	7	3	10
Chesterfield	8	4	2	2	11	8	10
Bournemouth	8	4	2	2	13	10	10

TUESDAY 2 OCTOBER 1973, EASTVILLE STADIUM

Bristol Rovers	1 – Warboys
Shrewsbury Town	0
Half-time:	1-0
Attendance:	11,455
Referee:	Anthony Glasson (Salisbury)
Bristol Rovers:	Eadie, Jacobs, Parsons, Green, Taylor, Prince, Stephens, Stanton, Warboys, Bannister, Dobson. Substitute: Fearnley
Shrewsbury Town:	Mulhearn, Gregory, Roberts, Matthias, Turner, Durban, Irvine, Calloway, Kearney, Tarbuck, Morris. Substitute: Bradley

Maurice Evans, manager of struggling Shrewsbury Town, promised Eastville fans that there would be no blanket defensive tactics from his side as they took on a Rovers side unbeaten in the League and without a goal against them in four games. Bottom club Shrewsbury made two changes to the side that drew 1-1 at home to Grimsby whilst Rovers were unchanged for the fifth successive game. Early on in the match Rovers' goals-against record looked gossamer thin, when first Alan Tarbuck sliced his shot wide with only Jim Eadie to beat and then Geoff Morris might have scored. When Morris sent in a waist-high drive from the left, Eadie was lying injured on the six-yard line and it was only the intervention of Trevor Jacobs, who threw himself down to divert the ball for a corner, that prevented a goal. Rovers' chances were being made through some delicate touches from Colin Dobson on the left and determined running by Bruce Bannister.

Kenny Stephens beats a lunge from Shrewsbury defender Roberts to cross a dangerous ball into the goalmouth.

Alan Warboys slides the ball past Shrewsbury goalkeeper Ken Mulhearn for Rovers' winning goal, with centre half Graham Turner beaten.

Alan Warboys got the all-important goal in the dying seconds of the first-half – under circumstances that led to Shrewsbury skipper Alan Durban, the former Derby midfield man, having his name taken as he continued to argue with the referee as the teams left the field. A throw from the touchline to Colin Dobson was driven low across the goalmouth to Warboys at the far post, who scored from close-range past Ken Mulhearn.

The second half revealed a bigger differential of talent between the teams, with one 10-minute spell of exhilarating Rovers approach work, but the finishing touches were not quite sharp enough despite all the fervent promptings of Frankie Prince, who was in fine form. Rovers' game began to flow and only a combination of determined individual tackles and a measure of luck saved Shrewsbury from a heavier defeat. As Rovers opened up a four-point gap over their rivals, manager Don Megson felt that it was time that the Bristol public were told 'a few home truths' following murmuring criticisms that Shrewsbury should have been more comprehensively beaten:

> When I played for Sheffield Wednesday in the First Division, a 1-0 win was treated like gold. In Bristol, if you don't win by three or four goals and take the mickey out of the opposition, they don't seem to think you have done a job. The public might as well know now they are not going to get the old-style Rovers pattern because that meant an exciting big win one week and a thumping the next. That's not what I'm after – for me the answer is 2-0 wins. They will point the way to promotion.

SATURDAY 6 OCTOBER 1973, VICARAGE ROAD, WATFORD

Watford	0
Bristol Rovers	0
Half-time:	0-0
Attendance:	10,202
Referee:	Bob Matthewson (Bolton)
Watford:	Rankin, Butler, Welbourne, Keen, Lees, Woodfield, Jennings, Bond, Morrissey, Lindsay, Farley. Substitute: Morgan for Farley (60 mins)
Bristol Rovers:	Eadie, Jacobs, Parsons, Green, Taylor, Prince, Stephens, Stanton, Warboys, Bannister, Dobson. Substitute: Fearnley

Rovers, with a four-point lead at the top of the table, met a rapidly improving Watford side managed by former Queens Park Rangers and Luton stalwart Mike Keen; they also included the League's leading goalscorer, Bill Jennings. Their substitute was Ian Morgan, signed on a month's loan from QPR. Rovers adopted an ultra-tight formation from the start, with flankmen Dobson and Stephens staying well back in the middle line, leaving Warboys and Bannister to fend for themselves up front. Rovers were soon under pressure and from a Bond free-kick touched to Morrissey, Keen's shot was just wide of Rovers' goal. However, from another free-kick at the other end Rovers could have snatched the lead. Stanton swept the ball wide to Warboys on the left and his low centre presented Bannister with a chance, but the striker completely miskicked and the chance was lost.

Rovers' defence again came under pressure when a fierce Farley shot grazed the bar, and Lindsay Parsons came to the away team's rescue with a superbly timed tackle just a few yards out from goal to rob Jimmy Lindsay following good approach work by Bond and Morrissey. Rovers were quick to give support to their twin strikers, creating chances for Taylor and one for Bannister that should have resulted in a goal. Stephens, energetic down the right, clipped over a perfect centre for Bannister, who headed wide from close range. Eadie prevented the first goal against Rovers in six games by sticking out his right leg to deflect a shot from Jennings away from low down inside the near post. As rain began to fall in the closing stages of the half, Eadie twice raced out to punch away crosses, but generally Rovers succeeded in their plan to smother Watford's attack.

Watford were first into the attack after the restart, but then Rovers went desperately close to taking the lead following an inspired run by Stephens. He glided past two defenders and hit in a fierce shot which Rankin did well to save. But the former Everton goalkeeper was unable to hold the ball, and as it rebounded off his shoulder Bannister followed up to shoot from close range. Rankin did brilliantly to keep the ball out and, as Bannister tried a second time, he hooked the ball across the face of the goal. Watford forced four corners in quick succession and nearly scored when Jennings ran in to meet Bond's free-kick, but the powerful header went into the side netting. Watford's biggest crowd of the season saw Rovers keep a clean sheet for the sixth successive week to give them the best goal average in the Football League.

SATURDAY 13 OCTOBER 1973, EASTVILLE STADIUM

Bristol Rovers	1 – Bannister
Port Vale	1 – McLaren
Half-time:	0-0
Attendance:	8,882
Referee:	Brian Daniels (Rainham)
Bristol Rovers:	Eadie, Jacobs, Parsons, Green, Taylor, Prince, Stephens, Stanton, Warboys, Bannister, Dobson. Substitute: Fearnley
Port Vale:	Boswell, Brodie, Lacey, Loska, Summerscales, Horton, Woodward, Tartt, McLaren, Mountford, Williams. Substitute: Gough for Williams (81 mins)

Rovers, unchanged for the eighth successive time, faced a Port Vale side seeking their first away win of the season, and the disappointingly small crowd saw the Potteries side kick-off towards the Tote End on a lush but greasy pitch. Adopting an adventurous 4-3-3 formation, it was Port Vale who threatened as once again Rovers were not as impressive before their own fans as they had

Bruce Bannister is hemmed in by Port Vale defenders, but still manages to get in a shot with Stuart Taylor backing him up.

been away from home. Bannister and Warboys foraged for openings and chased long balls from deep midfield without creating any clear-cut openings.

After 34 minutes Rovers should have taken the lead when Bannister hit over a low centre from the right, but Mike Green, who advanced into Vale's penalty area, mistimed his shot and sliced the ball well wide of the goal. Port Vale responded with a Brodie free-kick, following a foul by Parsons, with Mountford out-jumping the Rovers defence, but the striker headed just over the bar. Goalkeeper Alan Boswell made two good saves from Rovers' corners from the left and right, and the whistle blew for half-time before Stephens had the opportunity to take another flag kick.

Vale looked capable of stretching Rovers' defence as the second half got underway, but Jacobs and Prince and then Mike Green, made timely clearances. Rovers finally broke through after 59 minutes with a goal by Bannister, aided by his co-striker Warboys. From a corner on the left, Warboys met Dobson's corner kick and nodded it across to Bannister, who thrust his head forward to beat Boswell from close range.

Rovers almost added to their lead soon after from another Dobson corner, but Warboys' forceful header was headed over the bar by Tartt with the goalkeeper beaten. Vale hit back when Brodie shot just over the bar and Dobson went close to increasing Rovers' advantage with a low drive which was deflected inches wide of the post. Then, after 85 minutes, Rovers defence was finally breached for the first time in seven games. A long ball was punted down the field which glanced off Stuart Taylor's head as he and Mike Green went up for it. McLaren broke through and shook off a Lindsay Parsons challenge to beat Jim Eadie from close range. Megson, who before the game was presented with a giant bottle of whisky as Third Division Manager of the Month, admitted that Rovers looked tired and jaded, taking responsibility for the poor performance: 'With no midweek match to keep us on the boil, I decided to step up the training to pre-season standards, and I now believe I overdid it'.

Bruce Bannister beats Colin Tartt in the air to nod Alan Warboys' headed pass wide of Port Vale goalkeeper Alan Boswell to give Rovers the lead.

SATURDAY 20 OCTOBER 1973, EASTVILLE STADIUM

Bristol Rovers	0
York City	0
Half-time:	0-0
Attendance:	8,706
Referee:	Michael Taylor (Deal)
Bristol Rovers:	Eadie, Jacobs, Parsons, Green, Taylor, Prince, Stephens, Stanton, Warboys, Bannister, Dobson. Substitute: Fearnley
York City:	Crawford, Stone, Burrows, Lyons, Swallow, Topping, Pollard, Woodward, Calvert, Seal, Butler. Substitute: Peachey for Calvert (81 mins)

York City arrived at Eastville for Rovers' 2,000th League game, fourth in the table with only one defeat – 4-0 at Blackburn – in their previous nine games, bidding to keep a clean sheet for the sixth game in a row. Rovers, unchanged for the ninth successive game, were defending an unbeaten League record in this top-of-the-table clash. York, their massive defence guarding the Tote End goal in the first half, were quickly under pressure as Dobson weaved his way inside and flicked the ball to Warboys, but the centre forward sliced his shot wide. Almost immediately there was a remarkable escape for Rovers when Taylor slipped on the greasy surface and Seal darted past him to go clear. However, Rovers' centre half reached out while on the ground and brought him down 5yds outside the penalty area by grabbing the York striker's ankle. The referee assumed that Seal had slipped and refused to award a free-kick. Rovers, bringing wingers Stephens and Dobson into the game whenever possible, made little headway against York's towering defenders. A Prince shot following Stanton's free-kick was charged down in the crowded goalmouth and a Dobson flick from a Warboys header to the winger was saved by Crawford in the York goal.

The visitors moved forward with more purpose towards the end of the first half with Calvert meeting Stone's cross but sending his running header just wide, and with Rovers' defence looking more vulnerable, Eadie was twice forced to stretch for centres, while a Calvert shot struck Stuart Taylor's head and flashed just wide of the goal.

York, the most impressive visitors to Eastville of the season so far, kept up the standard in the early stages of the second half and put Rovers under pressure and Eadie was quick to kick the ball away from the feet of Seal as he bore down on goal. Rovers appealed for a penalty when a Dobson shot struck Topping's outstretched arms inside the box but the referee waved play to continue,

Kenny Stephens takes on the towering York City defence at Eastville.

and there were strong appeals again for a penalty as Bannister fell heavily as he was sandwiched between Burrows and Topping, but again the referee was unmoved. Late in the game Warboys was unlucky with a powerful header which grazed the bar following a Dobson free-kick. With honours shared in this often bruising goalless clash, there was little doubt that York City would be powerful challengers in the race to the Second Division. Rovers dropped their second point in successive home games, but kept their unbeaten record and the Third Division leadership.

WEDNESDAY 24 OCTOBER 1973, EDGAR STREET, HEREFORD

Hereford United	0
Bristol Rovers	0
Half-time:	0-0
Attendance:	12,501
Referee:	Derek Civil (Birmingham)
Hereford United:	Hughes, Mallender, Naylor, McLaughlin, Jones, Tavener, Evans, Owen, Lee, Gregory, Rudge. Substitute: Jenkins for Rudge (65 mins)
Bristol Rovers:	Eadie, Jacobs, Parsons, Green, Taylor, Prince, Stephens, Stanton, Warboys, Bannister, Dobson. Substitute: Fearnley for Stephens (65 mins)

In his programme notes, Hereford manager Colin Addison stated that this was the game that his side had all been looking forward to since their visit to Eastville six weeks previously. Addison considered Rovers had been 'a trifle lucky' to be able to boast an unbeaten record after his team had missed a late penalty and Rovers came back to claim a late draw in injury time. Rovers, unchanged for the tenth successive game, were bidding to re-establish a three-point lead in the Third Division as a fleet of Supporters' Club coaches and private cars followed the Pirates to Edgar Street. However, the first half provided little entertainment for the multitude of travelling fans, being described as a 'crashing bore' by Robin Perry reporting in the *Bristol Evening Post*. One of the best moves in the first half came from Hereford in the 9th minute when Alan Jones found a rare opening in the Rovers' defence, but Paul Lee failed to control the ball and the chance was lost. After 65 minutes of frustrating and disappointing football, in front of Hereford's biggest crowd of the season, the game came to life when both sides introduced substitutes. Gordon Fearnley took over from Kenny Stephens and Rovers started to click; when Tom Stanton pushed the ball through the middle, Bannister raced through and shot home, although his joy was short-lived as the linesman's flag went up for offside.

Two minutes later, a searing Alan Warboys cross-shot flew past Tommy Hughes but suffered a similar disappointment. Rovers should have clinched the match shortly after when the Hereford defence blundered for a third time. Gordon Fearnley broke clean through but, instead of shooting with the goal at his mercy, slipped the ball square to Warboys, who was standing in an offside position. If Fearnley had gone on he would have been a certain scorer. Warboys then had two

The controversial moment at Hereford when Bannister beats Tommy Hughes early in the second half, but is given offside.

further chances to win the game. At the other end, it needed a magnificent stop by Jim Eadie just 3 minutes from time to save Rovers from defeat. Bristol-born David Jenkins, who had come on as substitute, pierced Rovers' guard for the first time with a powerful header from Brian Evans' left-wing centre. Eadie, despite so little second-half activity, showed lightning reflexes and got down to scoop the ball away from just inside the post with a left-handed save. So Rovers maintained their unbeaten record in their first visit to Hereford in a game of energetic – and sometimes brutal – mediocrity, which trainer-coach Bobby Campbell described as 'the most physically punishing game he had watched in twelve years with the club'. The only consolation was that Rovers emerged with a point and that their thirteenth League game of the season was not all that unlucky.

SATURDAY 27 OCTOBER 1973, LEEDS ROAD, HUDDERSFIELD

Huddersfield Town	1 – Dolan
Bristol Rovers	2 – Warboys, Fearnley
Half-time:	0-2
Attendance:	9,532
Referee:	Roger Kirkpatrick (Leicester)
Huddersfield Town:	Poole, Hutt, Garner, Pugh, Saunders, Marshall, Smith, Gowling, Summerhill, Dolan, Hoy. Substitute: Chapman
Bristol Rovers:	Eadie, Jacobs, Parsons, Green, Taylor, Prince, Fearnley, Stanton, Warboys, Bannister, Dobson. Substitute: John (M)

Rovers made Colin Dobson skipper for the day on his return to his old club, with Don Megson making his first team change in eleven matches, Gordon Fearnley keeping his place at the expense of Kenny Stephens. It was Fearnley's first full League game of the season, although he had played in the League Cup defeat at Bournemouth and had been named as substitute twelve times. Huddersfield, unbeaten in seven games, were unchanged after the midweek win at Chesterfield.

Rovers, with only one goal to their credit from the previous four games, attacked from the kick-off in front off the largest Leeds Road crowd of the season and Warboys forced a corner in the opening seconds with a powerful charge down the right. Huddersfield hit back quickly and it took a superbly timed tackle by Frankie Prince to rob Hoy of the ball as he manoeuvred into a close-range shooting position. After 26 minutes Warboys put Rovers into the lead with a running header from a superbly flighted free-kick by Lindsay Parsons, after Prince had been brought down by Pugh just inside the Huddersfield half. Rovers went close to adding to their lead when Bannister hammered a shot at goal which Poole pushed away with difficulty. Fearnley tried to ram the ball home and his blocked shot spun out to Warboys, whose centre was parried by Poole and eventually scrambled clear.

Rovers didn't have to wait much longer for that second goal, which came after 35 minutes and was the first of the season for Fearnley. Awarded a free-kick on the left, as Dobson's kick came over Fearnley streaked into the goalmouth from the opposite flank to plant a firm header past Poole. Huddersfield made a determined start to the second half and won a free-kick just outside of Rovers' penalty area, but the resulting kick blasted at the defensive wall cannoned off Mike Green. Frankie Prince then received a booking for a remark he made after the referee had penalised Dobson. Huddersfield should have reduced Rovers' lead when Dolan darted in on a centre from the left by Alan Gowling, the former Manchester United player, but he sent his close-range header fractionally wide. Rovers still looked menacing despite Huddersfield's improved second-half showing, but their lead was cut after 64 minutes when they gave away a free-kick just outside the penalty area. Smith touched the ball a few yards to Dolan, who curled it round Rovers' wall and past the unsighted Eadie – only the second time in ten games that he had been beaten. Rovers fought back and in a frantic mêlée in the home team's goalmouth, Warboys, Fearnley and Bannister all had shots blocked. Dobson became the second Rovers player to be booked when he was cautioned for kicking the ball away. Rovers once again revealed in an away game a quality of all-round efficiency not seen yet this season at Eastville.

27 OCTOBER 1973

	P	W	D	L	F	A	Pts
ROVERS	14	8	6	0	18	5	22
Bournemouth	14	8	4	2	22	12	20
Oldham Athletic	14	6	7	1	15	8	19
York City	14	6	7	1	18	11	19
Hereford United	14	5	6	3	16	11	16
Wrexham	14	6	4	4	16	12	16

SATURDAY 3 NOVEMBER 1973, EASTVILLE STADIUM

Bristol Rovers	1 – Fearnley
Chesterfield	0
Half-time:	0-0
Attendance:	10,198
Referee:	Dennis Turner (Cannock)
Bristol Rovers:	Eadie, Jacobs, Parsons, Green, Taylor, Prince, Fearnley, Stanton, Warboys, Bannister, Dobson. Substitute: John (M)
Chesterfield:	Tingay, Tiler, Burton, Barlow, Winstanley, Stott, McHale, Moss, Large, Bellamy, Downes. Substitute: Ferris for Downes (52 mins)

Chesterfield manager Joe Shaw, who skippered Sheffield United when Rovers' manager was captain of Wednesday, brought his side to Eastville lying seventh in the table with an impressive record against the division's leading clubs. His team had beaten second-placed Bournemouth at Dean Court, drew away to third-placed Oldham and robbed fourth-placed York City of a home point. Gordon Fearnley retained his place in the side following his good performance at Huddersfield with Malcolm John again named as substitute. An early Chesterfield breakaway brought Eadie into action as he was forced to concede a corner to prevent Frank Large from turning in a header from a Moss cross. But in the main it was all Rovers, with goalkeeper Phil Tingay making three courageous saves during the opening 20 minutes, first to deny Fearnley a goal, then Warboys twice. A brilliant flicked pass by Bannister was back-heeled goalwards by Warboys but again Tingay saved smartly, then Bannister streaked through on a finely judged Dobson pass, cleverly beat Stott, but drove his shot just wide.

Gordon Fearnley is beaten to the ball by Chesterfield goalkeeper Phil Tingay.

Gordon Fearnley's downward header which Bruce Bannister followed into the net proved to be the only goal against Chesterfield.

Stanton and Prince were giving good support to a lively front line and Stanton hammered in a powerful drive that was blocked by Moss, and Stanton then shot high and wide after Warboys had powered his way past Winstanley and pushed a pass to Bannister. Then Stuart Taylor, up for a Stanton free-kick, headed past Tingay, but Bellamy hooked the ball off the line, and as a Fearnley corner from the right was partially cleared, Dobson went close with a studied chip shot which floated over the heads of Chesterfield's defence but dropped the wrong side of the crossbar. Five minutes from the break Fearnley had a chance to give Rovers the lead as Warboys and Bannister linked effectively, but he mistimed his shot and Tingay saved.

Rovers went straight back on the attack at the start of the second half, and Tingay plunged at Fearnley's feet as he moved on to a Warboys pass. As the game neared the hour mark, Dobson cleverly sent a spinning, half-volleyed pass to Warboys, who drove in a low shot on the turn which was just wide of the far post. For the first time Chesterfield came into the game as an attacking force, but Eadie remained untested. But with Bannister always threatening, Chesterfield were soon under pressure again, with a Warboys shot over the bar and a Stanton volley going high from a Dobson centre. The breakthrough finally came after 74 minutes when Gordon Fearnley ran in from the right to out-jump the Chesterfield defence and head in Parsons' raking cross.

Despite a week's concentration on shooting practice and laying siege to the Chesterfield goal for long periods, once again the front runners Warboys and Bannister were expected to break down a defence by themselves while their wingers flung over long balls. Frankie Prince and Tom Stanton formed a powerful midfield partnership for Rovers, driving forward to support an attack in which Dobson's subtle left-wing touches were so often complimentary to the strength of Warboys and the sharpness of Bannister. Rovers led the Third Division by three points, they and Leeds United in the First Division being the only unbeaten teams in the Football League. Rovers, who had conceded only five goals in fifteen games, also had the best defensive record in all four divisions.

SATURDAY 10 NOVEMBER 1973, FELLOWS PARK, WALSALL

Walsall	0
Bristol Rovers	0
Half-time:	0-0
Attendance:	6,058
Referee:	David Richardson (Clayton-le-Dale)
Walsall:	Kearns, Harrison, Fry, Young, Bennett, Robinson, Sloan, Fraser, Wright, Buckley, Atthey. Substitute: Shinton for Sloan (63 mins)
Bristol Rovers:	Eadie, Jacobs, Parsons, Green, Taylor, Prince, Stephens, Stanton, Warboys, Bannister, Dobson. Substitute: John (M) for Dobson (71 mins)

Kenny Stephens got a surprise recall against his former club as Gordon Fearnley went over on his ankle in training and aggravated an injury suffered against Chesterfield. Megson considered recalling Bryn Jones and also giving Malcolm John a chance, but thought that Stephens was best equipped to attack the left side of Walsall's defence. Rovers' other two doubtful players – Frankie

Alan Warboys
leaps for a header
in the goalless
draw at Walsall.

Prince (thigh strain) and Jim Eadie (flu) – both recovered. Walsall, with only one win in their last eight games, fielded the same side that lost narrowly at Grimsby on the previous Tuesday.

Although the game began in cheerful sunlight, heavy storms over lunchtime had left pools of water lying on the surface of the pitch. Rovers went straight into the attack, with a Parsons pass sending Warboys on a penetrating left-wing run. The striker's shot was deflected for a corner and Dobson's flag kick was headed away by Bennett. Parsons came to Rovers' rescue with a well-timed tackle, which brought Walsall a corner. Young's kick was headed out by Taylor, but the ball was pumped straight back into the goalmouth and Robinson shot straight at Eadie, who pushed the ball around the near post for another corner, which Rovers cleared. Walsall looked the sharper side and threatened again when Wright hit a powerful first-time shot on the turn which was just too high. Walsall should have taken the lead when a cross by Wright was chested down by Buckley to the feet of Sloan, but he rushed it and shot wide from only a few yards out. Rovers hit back as Dobson fired in a shot which grazed Walsall's crossbar and Warboys, from a Dobson free-kick, hammered a left-footed shot wide of Walsall's wall but Kearns made a smart save.

After 37 minutes the game erupted and Stephens' return to Fellows Park came to a premature end as he and Walsall's skipper Doug Fraser were sent off following a midfield brawl. The two players exchanged blows after clashing in a tackle, and despite the referee intervening and allowing play to continue the two players refused to heed the warning and immediately tangled again.

Walsall looked menacing in the early stages of the second-half with Harrison hitting a long shot over the bar, while a Wright free-kick flew wide of the post. Eadie was hurt as he clashed with Wright, but the referee refused to stop play as Rovers players surrounded their grounded goalkeeper, and eventually Eadie got up still grasping the ball and cleared it. After 71 minutes, Malcolm John made his first League appearance in two years when he was brought on as substitute for Colin Dobson. Rovers, roared on by a big following of supporters, almost snatched the lead when Prince's fierce 25yd drive was pushed over the bar by Kearns. Walsall hit back as Young hit an angled shot out of Eadie's reach, but Taylor hooked it away off Rovers' goal line.

Rovers were grateful to leave Fellows Park with their unbeaten run still intact. Megson rated it as the worst performance of the season, with no other team this term having created as many chances as Walsall's busy side.

TUESDAY 13 NOVEMBER 1973, EASTVILLE STADIUM

Bristol Rovers	3 – Warboys (3)
Southport	1 – Provan
Half-time:	1-1
Attendance:	10,472
Referee:	Peter Reeves (Leicester)
Bristol Rovers:	Eadie, Jacobs, Parsons, Green, Taylor, Prince, Stephens, Stanton, Warboys, Bannister, Dobson. Substitute: John (M)
Southport:	Taylor, O'Neil, Sibbald, Noble, Molyneux, Russell, Lee, Provan, Fryatt, Coleman, Clark. Substitute: Moore for Lee (75 mins)

Southport, the Division Four champions in 1972/73, finishing four points ahead of the rest of the field, were struggling to establish themselves in the higher division and arrived at Eastville languishing fourth from the bottom after sixteen games. Rovers had concerns about the fitness of a number of players for the midweek clash as Warboys had flu, John Rudge had a strained back, picked up playing against Spurs in Saturday's Combination match, and Gordon Fearnley was still under treatment for the ankle injury that kept him out of the team that played at Walsall. Frankie Prince had also suffered a recurrence of the thigh-muscle injury that troubled him in the previous match.

Rovers took the lead after 11 minutes when a mistake by Southport goalkeeper Alan Taylor let Warboys in for the opening goal. However, Southport were soon back on level terms equalising 9 minutes later from an Andy Provan free-kick.

In the second half, Warboys hammered home his second goal from a free-kick taken 10yds outside of the penalty area, and Rovers' top scorer had two chances to complete his hat-trick after he had given the home side the lead, but wasted both opportunities. He finally did manage to notch his hat-trick, 6 minutes from time, scoring with a right-foot drive after a solo run all the way from Rovers' penalty area, following a Southport corner. It was the third hat-trick of Warboys' career, the other two while he was with Cardiff City; he netted four times against Carlisle and three times against Preston. Rovers put Southport under constant pressure throughout the game, resulting in two cautions, for Noble and Russell, for their efforts to stop Rovers' rampant midfielders. Kenny Stephens enjoyed one of his best games with his lively running. If John Rudge had not been injured playing for the reserves, hat-trick-hero Warboys would not have appeared against Southport as under normal circumstances he would not have offered himself for selection, but with Fearnley already out of action and Rudge joining the injured list, Warboys said that he would play despite feeling 'really rough'. Commented manager Don Megson: 'If John Rudge had been fit, he would have played. Alan was not at all well and with the important Oldham game coming up so soon afterwards, I would have rested him against Southport'.

Alan Warboys drives in the first of his three goals scored in the 3-1 win over Southport.

SATURDAY 17 NOVEMBER 1973, BOUNDARY PARK, OLDHAM

Oldham Athletic	1 - Garwood
Bristol Rovers	1 – Green
Half-time:	1-0
Attendance:	11,018
Referee:	Edward Wallace (Crewe)
Oldham Athletic:	Ogden, Wood, Whittle, McNeil, Hicks, Mulvaney, McVitie, Jones, Lochhead, Garwood, Robins. Substitute: Hateley
Bristol Rovers:	Eadie, Jacobs, Parsons, Green, Taylor, Prince, Stephens, Stanton, Warboys, Bannister, Dobson. Substitute: John (M)

Rovers, who had been hit by a 'flu bug that had swept through the dressing rooms, reported no new victims on the morning of the top-of-the-table match, Warboys and Parsons declaring themselves fit to play, and were therefore unchanged after their 3-1 victory in midweek. However, Oldham had three men out through injury, including goalkeeper Harry Dowd.

Oldham were given a great boost in their bid to close the gap between themselves and Rovers when they took a 10th-minute lead through Colin Garwood, brought in for only his third game of the season. A through-ball from McVitie found Garwood, who beat Jacobs and hammered a right-footed shot into the roof of Rovers' net. It was only the third goal Rovers had conceded in an away game. Oldham, playing with tremendous flair and pace, looked a formidable side, but Rovers were by no means overrun and their simple, direct approach play caused plenty of anxiety for the home defence. Rovers replied with an attack led by Dobson down the left. He slipped a pass to Stanton, who found Bannister, but the striker's shot was deflected to Stephens and, as he hammered in a first-time attempt, Ogden turned the ball around for a corner, which was cleared. Oldham followed up their goal with a dangerous Wood free-kick after Mike Green had fouled Andy Lochhead, a Rovers' nemesis from his Aston Villa days. Taylor did well to get his head to the ball but could only turn it to Garwood, who shot wide. Kenny Stephens, in lively form, beat three men in a brilliant run, but his final centre was headed away by Hicks. Both teams were applauded off the field after 45 minutes of football which was well above the normal standard expected at a Third Division game.

Rovers made an impressive start to the second-half with two early corners but Oldham's imposing attack was soon in action again, with Garwood shooting straight at Eadie. After 57 minutes Warboys was booked for a clumsy foul on Hicks, and Stephens got himself in further trouble when

Mike Green clears an Oldham attack at Boundary Park, supported by Bannister, Warboys and Taylor.

Stuart Taylor gets the better of Oldham centre
forward Andy Lochhead on this occasion.

he was cautioned for showing dissent
following a disputed handball decision
in the Oldham goalmouth. Eadie rushed
out to kick the ball away from Garwood,
and Rovers immediately hit back when a
dangerous centre by Dobson flashed just
inches wide of the onrushing Warboys.

In the 73rd minute Mike Green became
the third Rovers player to be booked, for
arguing with the referee after he clashed
with Lochhead. Twelve minutes from the
end Rovers thought they had equalised
when Trevor Jacobs beat Ogden with a
superb shot, but the jubilation was short
lived when the referee disallowed the goal
because Warboys was in an offside position. But in the 81st minute Rovers did equalise when
captain Mike Green moved in on a Dobson free-kick from the left and headed past Ogden from
close range.

A 10-minute half-time pep talk from manager Don Megson reminding his players of the simple
footballing principles had transformed his team in the second-half, the improvement arresting
the initiative held by Oldham's talented team in the first-half. The draw enabled Rovers to keep
their unbeaten record in the eighteen League matches since the start of the season, equalling the
Third Division record. Only two other clubs – Plymouth in 1929 and Notts County in 1930 – had
achieved the same feat in the fifty-three-year history of the Third Division.

17 NOVEMBER 1973

	P	W	D	L	F	A	Pts
ROVERS	18	10	8	0	23	7	28
York City	18	8	9	1	21	11	25
Oldham Athletic	17	8	8	1	23	12	24
Bournemouth	18	9	6	3	26	16	24
Blackburn Rovers	18	9	3	6	31	23	21
Huddersfield Town	18	7	7	4	23	24	21

SATURDAY 24 NOVEMBER 1973, THE SPORTS GROUND, BIDEFORD, FA CUP 1ST ROUND

Bideford Town	0
Bristol Rovers	2 – Warboys, Bannister
Half-time:	0-0
Attendance:	4,800
Referee:	Alan Turvey (Basingstoke)
Bideford Town:	Lee, Morris, Hillson, May, Peterson, Gauntlett, Anthony, Rowe, Snell (S), Druce, Moxham. Substitute: Murphy for Morris (72 mins)
Bristol Rovers:	Eadie, Jacobs, Parsons, Green, Taylor, Prince, Fearnley, Stanton, Warboys, Bannister, Dobson. Substitute: John (M) for Fearnley (80 mins)

Bideford, from the First Division (South) of the Southern League, completed twelve matches in the
qualifying stages to eventually reach the first round proper of the FA Cup, which included five ties
against Falmouth Town and four matches against Trowbridge Town in the previous round.

Alan Warboys spins around after heading Rovers' first goal at Bideford, much to the delight of Stuart Taylor and Gordon Fearnley.

Bruce Bannister scores Rovers' second goal in the FA Cup clash with Bideford.

Rovers, not taking any liberties, made their customary cautious start, as if they were feeling out the strength of their part-time opponents. Bideford were first to threaten, but then Rovers cut loose with a slick move from Jacobs to Warboys to Dobson, but Bannister's final flicked shot went wide. Bannister had a half-chance of putting Rovers ahead when he seized on a Warboys pass, but teenage goalkeeper Lee beat the ball behind for a corner. Dobson's flag kick was met by Green, but his powerful header went wide of the far post. Bideford hit back and Eadie dived forward to smother an angled shot by Moxham, then, after a handball by Parsons, Prince flung himself full-length to head clear Morris's free-kick.

Bideford were holding their own quite comfortably and almost snatched the lead after 32 minutes. The lively Druce darted past Parsons and hit over a low cross from the right, which only needed a touch to stab the ball home. But Gauntlett, with one eye on the onrushing Eadie, failed to connect and the ball flashed across Rovers' goalmouth. The near miss lifted Bideford and they hit at Rovers again, Snell's header going just wide of the near post, Green clearing the ball for a corner to rob the darting Druce, and Snell heading over the bar from Rowe's pass. Bideford were cheered back to the dressing room after a polished performance in the goalless first half.

Rovers made a businesslike start to the second half, no doubt prompted by some sharp comments from the manager, and Prince's first-time shot, following a pass from Bannister, sailed over Bideford's bar. Three minutes into the second half, Rovers broke through a stubborn home guard to take the lead through Warboys' tenth goal of the season. Bannister, trying to hustle in from the left, was fouled by Anthony 10yds outside the penalty area. Dobson floated the free-kick into the goalmouth where Warboys out-jumped a mass of Bideford defenders to head past Lee.

Bideford were unruffled by the setback and plugged away at Rovers' defence. Rovers should have increased their lead when a lobbed Stanton pass put Bannister clear, but the striker shot against the onrushing Lee and as the ball rebounded to him, his second attempt was deflected for a corner. Rovers increased their lead after 73 minutes when Warboys' heading power again shattered the home side, providing the opportunity for Bannister to prod the ball home from close range.

With Bideford taking the plaudits after the game, Don Megson criticised his side for the hard work they made of winning the FA Cup tie, commenting that, 'our display was the poorest advertisement for League football, and if we produced this sort of stuff in the Third Division, we wouldn't win a match'.

SATURDAY 1 DECEMBER 1973, GOLDSTONE GROUND, BRIGHTON

Brighton & Hove Albion	2 – O'Sullivan, Howell
Bristol Rovers	8 – Warboys (4), Bannister (3), Fearnley
Half-time:	1-5
Attendance:	10,762
Referee:	Tommy Dawes (Norwich)
Brighton & Hove Albion:	Powney, Templeman, Ley, Spearitt, Gall, Howell (R), Towner, Beamish, Hilton, Robertson, O'Sullivan. Substitute: Howell (G) for Ley (45 mins)
Bristol Rovers:	Eadie, Jacobs, Parsons, Green, Taylor, Prince, Fearnley, Stanton, Warboys, Bannister, Dobson. Substitute: John (M)

The *Football League Review* magazine included with the Brighton programme contained a special feature about Bristol Rovers, with a colour picture of a smiling Bruce Bannister and Alan Warboys. The Commentary feature in the programme welcomed the visitors, remarking somewhat prophetically that 'All the signs are of an entertaining match...' The Pirates arrived at the Goldstone Ground for a 2 p.m. kick-off, an hour earlier than usual, to save electricity during the Miners' Strike, and the subsequent ban on the use of floodlights. Because of the poor weather conditions a number of matches were postponed resulting in the television cameras rushing down to Brighton to feature the game on *The Big Match* the following day. Possibly because of the difficulty black and white television viewers would have distinguishing between the blue-and-white-striped shirts of Brighton and Rovers' normal change strip of red-and-white-stripes, the visitors borrowed a set of gold shirts from the hosts. Brighton, under new boss Brian Clough, humiliated midweek 4-0 by amateurs Walton & Hersham in the FA Cup, made three changes following the Cup debacle. It was a cold but sunny afternoon – Rovers had the sun behind them in the first half – and the pitch had a soft surface but was hard underneath.

Brighton made a promising start and Stanton was forced to concede an early corner, but it was Rovers who went ahead after only 4 minutes with a superbly worked goal by Bannister. Parsons and Dobson combined to work the ball to Warboys on the left and the big striker eased past Gall and hit over a low cross which Bannister stabbed in from close range.

Eight minutes later Rovers scored again; it was Warboys and Dobson who executed the opening and from Dobson's cross, Fearnley planted a running header deep into the far corner of the goal. Brighton fought back and cut Rovers' lead in the 19th minute when O'Sullivan beat Eadie with a low shot struck from outside the penalty area. But it was a temporary respite for the home team and Rovers opened up a 3-1 lead when Bannister scored again with a well-placed header after Jacobs had overlapped down the right and hit over a centre. Two minutes later it was 4-1 as Bannister completed his first Rovers hat-trick. Awarded a free-kick just outside Brighton's penalty area, Warboys took it and smashed a shot

Bruce Bannister and Gordon Fearnley celebrate Rovers' first goal of eight scored past Brighton goalkeeper Brian Powney.

Alan Warboys and Tom Stanton congratulate Bannister, centre, on his opening goal.

past the Brighton wall, which Powney got his chest behind, but couldn't hold and Bannister was there to tuck home the rebound. Rovers scored once more before the interval and again much of the credit was due to the intelligent accuracy of Dobson's crossing. This time it was Warboys who headed past Powney to complete a great move instigated by a finely judged long pass out of defence by Prince.

Brighton were quickly under pressure again at the start of the second half, and it took a brilliant one-handed save by Powney to keep out Stanton's fierce drive. After 55 minutes Warboys ran on to a perfect Bannister through-ball to steer the ball past the luckless Powney to make it 6-1. Amazingly Rovers had taken every chance that came their way. Dobson then hooked a centre over the bar, while a save from Powney denied Bannister a fourth goal. After 63 minutes Brighton's defence was split by a long Parsons clearance and Warboys was on to it to beat the advancing Powney to become the second Rovers player of the afternoon to complete a hat-trick. In the 70th minute, with Brighton's defence strung out hoping for an offside decision, Warboys eased through to make it 8-1 with a coolly taken goal. Three minutes from the end Brighton became the first team to score two goals against Rovers when Ronnie Howell turned in a low centre past Eadie. Rovers' retort was swift, but they were denied a ninth goal as Warboys hammered a cross-shot on to Brighton's bar.

Despite Brighton's biggest ever home defeat, the crowd, including an enthusiastic contingent from Bristol, gave the visitors a rousing ovation at the end of a momentous match in the history of Bristol Rovers. Meanwhile back at Eastville, Rovers Reserves gave their best display of the season with a crushing 6-1 win over... Bristol City Reserves.

A Record Day

Rovers created a new Third Division record by going unbeaten for nineteen games from the start of the season.

Warboys and Bannister became the first players to both score hat-tricks in the same League game for Rovers. This was Bannister's only League hat-trick for Rovers.

Rovers had never scored eight goals in a League match before, while Brighton became the first side to score two goals against Rovers that season.

SATURDAY 8 DECEMBER 1973, EASTVILLE STADIUM	
Bristol Rovers	4 – Warboys (3, 1 penalty), Jacobs
Southend United	0
Half-time:	0-0
Attendance:	10,778
Referee:	Roger Perkin (Stafford)
Bristol Rovers:	Eadie, Jacobs, Parsons, Green, Taylor, Prince, Fearnley, Stanton, Warboys, Bannister, Dobson. Substitute: Rudge for Parsons (80 mins)
Southend United:	Bellotti, Moody, Ford, Elliott, Townsend, Worthington, Booth, Brace, Guthrie, Coulson, Johnson. Substitute: Moore for Brace (82 mins)

Southend, the last team to beat Rovers in a League game (they won 2-1 at Eastville in March 1973), featured a number of recent signings in their squad following the sale of Peter Taylor to Crystal Palace in October. Rovers, not surprisingly, kept the same side that played at Brighton, but included John Rudge as substitute for his first taste of League football that season.

Rovers, playing into a stiff breeze for the first half, went straight on the attack and as Fearnley stormed in towards the far post Dobson's cross was headed clear by Ford. An ill-judged clearance by Moody was blocked by Bannister and the ball slipped to Warboys, whose fierce cross-shot was collected at the second attempt by Bellotti. Southend were under further pressure when Bellotti pushed out a hooked shot by Dobson and as the ball came down to Warboys, Worthington cleared off the line. Rovers should have taken the lead after 31 minutes when Dobson's floating free-kick to the far post was headed over by Stuart Taylor. There were further narrow escapes for Southend before the interval with Booth, Worthington and Elliott all clearing off the goal line.

Rovers finally made the breakthrough just 2 minutes after the restart as Warboys hammered home his fifteenth goal of the season. Dobson's centre from the left was headed down by Warboys to Bannister, who laid the ball back to Warboys, who beat Bellotti with a powerful, low shot. Southend hit straight back and were denied by a magnificent Eadie save, who deflected the ball around the post with his fingertips. Brace then headed past Eadie, from a Moody free-kick, but the linesman's flag was up for offside. The second Rovers' goal arrived after 64 minutes. Prince won the ball just inside Southend's half and sent Dobson away to the left. Rovers' winger turned the ball perfectly inside to Warboys who gave Bellotti no chance with a well-controlled shot. As Rovers kept up the pressure they won another corner on the left, and when Dobson curled his kick into the area the ball was punched out by Guthrie, who had come back to mark Taylor. Bannister, Rovers' official penalty taker, allowed Warboys to take the spot kick and he cracked the ball into the top corner of the net. It was the striker's second hat-trick in successive games and boosted his tally for the season to seventeen.

Ten minutes from the end Parsons went down injured and was replaced by Rudge, who took up a midfield position with Stanton dropping back to left-back. After 87 minutes Rovers should have had a second penalty when Fearnley was brought down by Worthington a good yard inside the penalty area, but the referee awarded a free-kick just outside the area and Rovers made a mess of their set-piece routine. As the game moved into injury time, Trevor Jacobs netted his first goal for the club when he ran straight through an advancing Southend defence and floated the ball over the 'keeper, who was too far off his line. Even though Warboys' goals took the headlines, Megson reminded supporters that, 'It is important to the club that every player's contribution is recognised'.

Mike Green had an outstanding game in Rovers' back four; Jim Eadie made a magnificent save when only a goal in front; Tom Stanton had a fine first half; and Frankie Prince took the midfield honours in the sparkling second half.

Alan Warboys completes his second hat-trick in successive games, beating Southend goalkeeper Derek Bellotti with a penalty.

Jim Eadie gathers the ball safely as Stuart Taylor holds off Southend striker Chris Guthrie.

SATURDAY 15 DECEMBER 1973, COUNTY GROUND, NORTHAMPTON, FA CUP 2ND ROUND

Northampton Town	1 – Buchanan
Bristol Rovers	2 – Warboys, Fearnley
Half-time:	1-2
Attendance:	6,181
Referee:	Jim Bent (Hemel Hempstead)
Northampton Town:	Starling, Tucker, Neal, Clarke, Robertson, Gregory, Felton, Best, Buchanan, Buck, Stratford. Substitute: Oman
Bristol Rovers:	Eadie, Jacobs, Parsons, Green, Taylor, Prince, Fearnley, Stanton, Warboys, Bannister, Dobson. Substitute: Rudge

For Rovers' former manager, Bill Dodgin senior, now chief scout with the club, the FA Cup tie at Fourth Division Northampton Town had a special attraction. The new Northampton manager, Bill Dodgin junior, was his son, and Dodgin junior's assistant was former Rovers wing-half John Petts. After an Eastville playing career in which Petts contributed a great deal towards the development of young players in addition to his performances on the field, he had spells as player-manager of Bath City and Trowbridge Town before linking up with Dodgin at the start of the 1973/74 season. Rovers, hit by an injury crisis before the match, had Warboys, Bannister, Parsons and Eadie on the treatment table on the Friday, but all were declared fit, if not 100 per cent, and Rovers fielded the same line-up that crushed Brighton and Southend. The County Ground pitch was in excellent condition, but it was a grey and cold afternoon.

Rovers' menacing forward duo were soon in action and after 8 minutes Warboys struck to put Rovers ahead. Parsons started the move with a long clearance which Bannister turned out to Fearnley, and as the centre came over Warboys jumped to head the ball over the outstretched hands of Starling.

By the 15th minute the Cobblers were on terms. Stratford took a pass from Felton, got around the Rovers defence and pulled back a centre which Buchanan smashed past Eadie. Northampton

Alan Warboys scores Rovers' first goal against Northampton Town.

Gordon Fearnley challenges two Northampton defenders for the ball, while Warboys watches proceedings.

then began to look the more menacing side and Eadie had to pull off two saves from Stratford and Best, with Felton's crosses causing problems for Rovers' defence as Northampton continued to dominate. But then a slip by Starling enabled Rovers to snatch the lead against the run of play. The Northampton goalkeeper failed to hold a free-kick from Green and Fearnley darted in to stab home an easy goal. After 40 minutes Stratford again had the ball in Rovers' net, but the goal was disallowed for an obstruction offence on Eadie. Three minutes later Stanton was booked for a tackle on Buchanan, and just before half-time Eadie needed two attempts to gather a low shot from future Liverpool full-back Phil Neal.

When the teams came out for the second half, Warboys had his right thigh heavily bandaged. He and Bannister were left to fend for themselves with Dobson dropping back to help Parsons cope with the dangerous Felton. Rovers should have increased their lead when Jacobs charged through a gap but he floated his shot over the out-rushing Starling and over the bar too.

The Third Division leaders were somewhat fortunate to remain ahead when Stratford's centre flashed across a gaping goalmouth and was completely missed by Buck. Felton ran in on the far post and hit a shot which Eadie kicked off the line as he fell backwards. Minutes later Stratford got the ball past Eadie, but the goal was disallowed for offside, and Northampton went close to equalising when another Felton centre was headed just wide by Best. Eight minutes from the end, Parsons became the second Rovers player to be booked after he had brought down Felton – his third caution of the season.

Rovers' progress to the third round was overshadowed by some ugly crowd behaviour which threatened to end the match. The flashpoint came when referee Jim Bent disallowed Stratford's effort and home fans invaded the pitch. This was the signal for Rovers' fans to come over the barriers and fights broke out on the edge of the pitch. Order was eventually restored after the referee threatened to abandon the game.

SATURDAY 22 DECEMBER 1973, ABBEY STADIUM, CAMBRIDGE

Cambridge United	2 – Greenhalgh (2)
Bristol Rovers	2 – Stanton, Warboys
Half-time:	1-1
Attendance:	4,491
Referee:	Robin Clay (Gainsborough)
Cambridge United:	Vasper, O'Donnell, Akers, Guild, Eades, Rathbone, Ferguson, Greenhalgh, Simmons, Lennard, Watson. Substitute: Lill for Rathbone (81 mins)
Bristol Rovers:	Eadie, Jacobs, Parsons, Green, Taylor, Prince, Fearnley, Stanton, Warboys, Bannister, Dobson. Substitute: Rudge

Rovers, bidding for their second double of the season on their first-ever trip to third from bottom Cambridge United, were again unchanged, including full-back Parsons who had only taken part in one training session during the week – on the Friday before the game.

The pitch at the tidy Cambridge ground was immaculate but Rovers were playing straight into a dazzling sun, and during the lively start almost conceded an own-goal by Prince. Rovers took an 8th-minute lead with virtually their first strike at goal, and it came after they had soaked up early pressure by a busy home team. Green squared a free-kick to Jacobs, who centred into the penalty area from the right. Warboys headed back to Stanton, who beat Vasper with a low, first-time shot. Cambridge kept Rathbone, Eades and Guild bunched together in middle of their back line but were unable to prevent Warboys from flicking a Fearnley pass into the net, but the goal was disallowed for offside.

Eadie then rescued Rovers with a fine save. Watson's shot was blocked by Stanton and Lennard hit in a powerful drive as the ball rebounded to him, but Eadie dived full-length to his right to make a snatching save. After 30 minutes United's enterprise was rewarded with an equaliser by Greenhalgh, who took possession of the ball inside the centre circle and ran straight through the middle. As three Rovers' defenders converged on him he stabbed the ball to Ferguson, took a quick return pass and shot past Eadie.

Rovers, who had been caught frequently by United's offside trap in the first half, seemed unable to come up with a solution during the half-time tactics talk. They had a chance to regain the lead when the length of Eadie's clearance from his hands took United's defence by surprise and Warboys forged his way through, but he shot wide. There was another half-chance allowed to go begging after Warboys had been brought down by Lennard. Dobson chipped the free-kick to Taylor, who just failed to make contact. Rovers eventually regained the lead 11 minutes from the end with Warboys' seventeenth League goal of the season. Jacobs started the move with a pass to Stanton, who pushed the ball on to Bannister. Warboys, after receiving his well-placed pass, fired a shot past Vasper, who might have done better to keep it out. In the 81st minute Greenhalgh scored his second goal of the game as Cambridge equalised, when he got his head to a fiercely driven left-foot shot from Watson to leave Eadie helpless. Rovers almost snatched a winner when Taylor's header from a Dobson corner beat Vasper, but was kneed off the line by Akers.

There was little sign at the Abbey Stadium of the lethal finishing power that rocked Brighton and Southend, and neither was there the defensive solidarity that had been the basis of the successful first half of the season. The way the game went, it seemed a possibility that Cambridge would cause the shock of the day by wrecking Rovers unbeaten League run. That didn't happen mainly because Rovers' midfield men, Stanton and Prince, made a massive contribution.

WEDNESDAY 26 DECEMBER 1973, EASTVILLE STADIUM

Bristol Rovers	4 – Warboys (2), Bannister, Taylor
Plymouth Argyle	2 – Hore, Mariner
Half-time:	2-1
Attendance:	22,353
Referee:	John Gow (Swansea)
Bristol Rovers:	Eadie, Jacobs, Parsons, Green, Taylor, Prince, Fearnley, Stanton, Warboys, Bannister, Dobson. Substitute: Rudge
Plymouth Argyle:	Furnell, Randall, Sullivan, Hore, Saxton, Hague, Welsh, Davey, Mariner, Machin, Rogers. Substitute: Rickard

Plymouth Argyle's League position as the halfway point of the season approached was a disappointment for the Pilgrims' manager, Tony Waiters, the former Blackpool and England goalkeeper. But despite their mid-table position, Rovers expected a hard game from a talented Plymouth side that included Paul Mariner, the goalscoring success of the season, his first in League football. Rovers were unchanged for the fifth successive game, John Rudge continuing as substitute. The 22,353 attendance for the West Country Boxing Day clash was Eastville's biggest for a Third Division match since Aston Villa's visit in January 1971, which attracted a crowd of 25,636.

Bruce Bannister scores his ninth goal of the season in the Boxing Day goal-feast against Plymouth Argyle.

Stuart Taylor just beats Plymouth Argyle's talented teenager Paul Mariner to the ball.

Rovers fell behind in the 13th minute to a savagely struck shot from Plymouth's longest-serving player, John Hore. The well-deserved equaliser came in the 25th minute from the head of Stuart Taylor after Alan Warboys had set off on a powerful run and won a corner kick. Gordon Fearnley's set-piece found Taylor in the Plymouth goalmouth, who planted a firm header past goalkeeper Jim Furnell. Seven minutes later Rovers were in front. Frankie Prince found Dobson in space on the left flank with a raking pass. Tom Stanton challenged for the ball with goalkeeper Furnell as the winger's cross came over and as the ball ran loose, Warboys bundled it over the line. Rovers increased their lead after 51 minutes with Bruce Bannister's ninth goal of the season. Gordon Fearnley advanced down the right wing and whipped in a cross for Warboys to nod down for Bannister to score his eighth League goal of the campaign.

It should have been plain sailing from then on, but Bristol's best gate of the season witnessed Rovers' most embarrassing 20 minutes for a very long time, coming midway through the second half with the home side leading 3-1. Suddenly Argyle were so firmly in control that it seemed inevitable that the margin would be narrowed. Fortunately for Rovers, it was not until 13 minutes from the end that Paul Mariner – an immensely promising twenty-year-old – slotted home Neil Hague's low cross past Eadie to make it 3-2. Time enough to save a point, but Rovers at last realised the possible cost of their surrender of the midfield to Ernie Machin, who had been the general behind his side's resurgence. He now found those gaping holes were being filled by Rovers' men.

Just before the end, free-scoring centre forward Warboys struck again after being put through by a fine Tommy Stanton pass. His second goal of the game put him on a total of twenty-one for the season, and there was a belief amongst Rovers' fans that he was all set to strongly challenge Alfie Bigg's club record of thirty-seven in a season. The defeat of Plymouth stretched the Eastville club's run of unbeaten League games to twenty-seven, matching their historic achievement of 1952/53 when they went on to claim the Division Three (South) championship. The Boxing Day takings of over £9,000 smashed Rovers' record for a League match, previously £7,400 from the encounter with Aston Villa in January 1971, and put the club in their healthiest financial situation for years.

SATURDAY 29 DECEMBER 1973, EASTVILLE STADIUM

Bristol Rovers	1 – Wigginton (own goal)
Grimsby Town	1 – Lewis
Half-time:	1-1
Attendance:	14,317
Referee:	Arthur Hart (Borough Green)
Bristol Rovers:	Eadie, Jacobs, Parsons, Green, Taylor, Prince, Fearnley, Stanton, Warboys, Bannister, Dobson. Substitute: Rudge
Grimsby Town:	Wainman, Beardsley, Booth, Chatterley, Wigginton, Gray, Barton, Hickman, Lewis, Boylen, Sharp. Substitute: Fletcher

Grimsby centre half Clive Wigginton (right) deflects the ball past his own goalkeeper, Wainman, from a Bannister centre for Rovers' goal.

Winger Colin Dobson attempts a shot at the Grimsby goal during the game at Eastville.

Grimsby Town's mid-table position was due mainly to the fact that they had found scoring a difficult job, particularly away from home. However, they arrived at Eastville having gained a point at third-placed York on Boxing Day, and although they had won only once on their travels, their away defensive record was second only to Rovers. Tom Stanton came through a morning fitness test and Rovers were unchanged for the seventh successive game. Another good crowd saw Rovers kick towards the Muller Road end in the first-half on a pitch that was well sanded through the middle. Rovers moved straight into the attack from the kick-off and Warboys had two opportunities to score before they took the lead after only 6 minutes. Stanton slipped a pass out to Bannister on the left and as his centre came over Wigginton, mindful of Warboys' presence, failed to connect properly with the cross and it glanced off the top of his head into the far corner of the net, well out of Wainman's reach.

Shortly after, Rovers went close to adding a second goal when Bannister nodded down a Dobson centre to Green, whose first-time shot on the turn brought a smart save from Wainman. Grimsby settled down and Barton was only a yard short of touching in an equaliser as he just failed to make contact with Booth's low drive. Warboys cut loose again and brought a roar from the crowd as he lashed a tremendous shot into the net off the underside of the bar. However, the goal was disallowed for offside.

Grimsby should have equalised when Green allowed Lewis to accelerate past him, but the centre forward shot over the bar from close range. Rovers surrendered their lead after 27 minutes when a slapdash backpass from Mike Green was seized on by Lewis, who just beat the out-rushing Eadie and slotted in from an acute angle. Rovers were again in trouble early in the second half when the lively Lewis threatened with a penetrating run, but was halted by Taylor's tackle.

Rovers should have regained the lead when a Jacobs drive across the penalty area was teed up by Dobson for Fearnley, whose shot was hit straight at Wainman. Fearnley wasted another chance, following a Parsons free-kick, shooting over the bar from 10yds. In the dying minutes there was an anxious moment for Rovers as Grimsby broke away to force two corners on the right, but Eadie eventually dealt with the threat. Despite a rather jaded performance by Rovers their hard-won point against a workmanlike Grimsby increased their lead to four points and created a new Third Division record by playing twenty-eight consecutive League games without defeat.

29 DECEMBER 1973

	P	W	D	L	F	A	Pts
ROVERS	23	13	10	0	42	14	36
Bournemouth	23	13	6	4	32	18	32
York City	22	10	11	1	29	14	31
Chesterfield	23	11	7	5	25	18	29
Wrexham	23	11	6	6	31	20	28
Huddersfield Town	23	10	8	5	32	26	28

TUESDAY 1 JANUARY 1974, THE VALLEY, CHARLTON

Charlton Athletic	1 – Curtis (penalty)
Bristol Rovers	1 – Rudge
Half-time:	0-1
Attendance:	11,414
Referee:	Ron Crabbe (Devon)
Charlton Athletic:	Dunn, Curtis, Tumbridge, Smart, Goldthorpe, Reeves, Hales, Flanagan, Horsfield, Dunphy, Peacock. Substitute: Powell for Smart (81 mins)
Bristol Rovers:	Eadie, Jacobs, Parsons, Green, Taylor, Prince, Fearnley, Stanton, Rudge, Bannister, Dobson. Substitute: Jones

Rovers went into their first game of the New Year against high-scoring Charlton Athletic without leading scorer Alan Warboys, sidelined by the recurrence of an injury to his right leg. It was the first game he had missed since being signed in March 1973, but it gave John Rudge his first chance of the season since suffering an injury in the Watney Cup tie against West Ham two weeks before the start of the League programme.

In the early stages of the match, despite a high work-rate throughout the side, the ball never seemed to fall for Rovers and they fell behind to a 31st-minute penalty by Curtis. Eamon Dunphy, the stylish midfield general of Athletic's side, tired of seeing his service to forwards destroyed by the resolute play of Rovers defenders, edged through on his own, but Trevor Jacobs, covering well, put too much of his body into the challenge and fouled Dunphy. Full-back Bob Curtis cracked in the spot kick.

Charlton's penalty goal upset Rovers' rhythm, but they hit back in the second half. Colin Dobson came out after the interval with a strapping on his left ankle, but he showed no adverse effects and played a leading role in Rovers' revival, together with Frankie Prince. In the 67th minute, Dobson floated an accurate free-kick from the left and Rudge rose above the defence and sent an unstoppable header beyond the reach of former Aston Villa goalkeeper John Dunn. Rudge, well supported by Bannister throughout the match, hammered a shot against the post with Dunn beaten, but the ball bounced back to the waiting arms of the goalkeeper. He was then foiled by a save from the Charlton goalkeeper which surprised Dunn as much as anyone. Bruce Bannister had a late chance to earn Rovers their sixth away win of the season, but he finished his run in the last minute of the game with a shot straight at the goalkeeper.

The absence of prolific scorer Alan Warboys could have proved a handicap for Rovers to hold on to their unbeaten record. In fact, against one of the division's better sides, it brought to light resources that had remained hidden while his dynamic exploits had hogged the headlines. Playing in his first game League game since April 1973, John Rudge used all his guile to lead an attack that produced a tremendous variety of approach routes as an alternative to the power and strength of Warboys.

SUNDAY 6 JANUARY 1974. CITY GROUND, NOTTINGHAM. FA CUP 3RD ROUND

Nottingham Forest	4 – Martin (2), Chapman, Lyall
Bristol Rovers	3 – Prince, Dobson, Rudge
Half-time:	2-1
Attendance:	23,456
Referee:	John Hunting (Leicester)
Nottingham Forest:	Barron, O'Kane, Winfield, Chapman, Cottam, Hindley, McKenzie, Lyall, Martin, O'Neill, Bowyer. Substitute: Dennehy for Hindley (67 mins)
Bristol Rovers:	Eadie, Jacobs, Parsons, Green, Taylor, Prince, Fearnley, Stanton, Rudge, Bannister, Dobson. Substitute: Jones for Dobson (84 mins)

NOTTINGHAM FOREST FOOTBALL CLUB

Official Team Sheet

FOOTBALL ASSOCIATION CHALLENGE CUP
ROUND THREE

SUNDAY, 6th JANUARY, 1974—CITY GROUND

NOTTM. FOREST		BRISTOL ROVERS
Red Shirts / White Shorts		Blue/White Quarters / White Shorts
Jim Barron	1	Jim Eadie
Liam O'Kane	2	Trevor Jacobs
John Winfield	3	Lindsay Parsons
Peter Hindley	4	Mike Green
John Cottam	5	Stuart Taylor
Paul Richardson	6	Frankie Prince
Duncan McKenzie	7	Gordon Fearnley
George Lyall	8	Tom Stanton
Neil Martin	9	Alan Warboys
Martin O'Neill	10	Bruce Bannister
Ian Bowyer	11	Colin Dobson
Tommy Jackson	12	John Rudge

REFEREE   **Mr. J. HUNTING** (Leicester)
LINESMEN   **Mr. P. J. RICHARDSON** (Lincoln)
Mr. G. A. ROSE (Leicester)

45p.

THANK YOU FOR YOUR SUPPORT!

Rovers' first-ever Sunday match was played against Nottingham Forest in the FA Cup. Clubs were not permitted to charge admission, hence the price of the official team sheet, which had to be bought to enter the ground. The cost of the match programme was 6p.

For the first time, the draw for the 3rd Round proper of the FA Cup was made in the BBC television studios. The draw was brought forward to Saturday afternoon from its usual Monday lunchtime, not for the benefit of supporters, but for the Football Pools firms who were likely to have printing problems due to the power crisis. Sunday 6 January was an historic day for British professional football, with four FA Cup ties being played, all welcomed by large attendances. The first-ever Sunday match kicked off at 11 o'clock at Cambridge, where 8,479 people, easily the club's best crowd of the season, saw the home team draw 2-2 with Oldham. Nearly 40,000 people saw the tie at Bolton v. Stoke – a staggering 20,000 above the normal gate figures of the Lancashire club. Rovers' tie with Forest was one of the four groundbreaking matches, and the first time Rovers played a Sunday game.

Second Division Forest showed their power from the start and carried out their threat of an all-out attack from the opening moments. Neil Martin put them in front after only 2 minutes following a fine move between Duncan McKenzie, John Winfield and Ian Bowyer. Winfield hit a long pass from left to right and when Bowyer lofted the ball into the middle, an unmarked Martin hooked the ball past Eadie into the net. After taking some time to settle, Rovers had the Forest defence in trouble with a one-two between Bannister and Rudge, which ended with Rudge shooting inches over the bar. Cottam then shot over the Rovers bar when Jim Eadie failed to hold a George Lyall free-kick, and then Forest went two goals up with more inspired football from Chapman and Bowyer. Eadie could only palm out a centre by Bowyer, when he might have caught the ball, which rolled to Bob Chapman who hammered it low into the net from 20yds. Rovers, rather over-awed at this stage, got the break they needed with the last kick of the first half, Frankie Prince lofting an angled shot from the left over goalkeeper Jim Barron. From their first corner of the game, in the 51st minute, Rovers equalised. Gordon Fearnley took the kick and Barron pushed the ball weakly out to Colin Dobson, who drove home a great shot from 14yds.

Colin Dobson shoots through a crowded penalty area to score Rovers' second goal from a corner. Stuart Taylor and Mike Green are also in the picture.

John Rudge cracks the ball past Nottingham Forest goalkeeper Jim Barron to give Rovers a 3-2 lead in the Sunday FA Cup tie.

Ten minutes later, Bannister cleverly spotted an opening and sent Rudge away to score, picking his spot as Barron left his line. Suddenly Forest were looking a very ordinary side and when Miah Dennehy, a future Rovers player, came on for the injured Peter Hindley it looked as though Manchester City were all set for a visit to Eastville.

However, 10 minutes from the end, Stuart Taylor tripped George Lyall in the penalty area and the outstanding midfielder in Forest's purple patch took the kick himself to make it 3-3. Forest staged a final rally and 3 minutes later Lyall's corner was headed on by John Cottam for Neil Martin to scramble in the winner. A crowd twice the size of Forest's average gate gave a standing ovation to both teams at the end of a superb cup tie. Forest were just the better controlled and more skilful side, but there was not a lot in it with Rovers growing in stature as the game wore on. This was the highest score against Rovers this season and only their second defeat.

SATURDAY 12 JANUARY 1974, THE SHAY, HALIFAX

Halifax Town	0
Bristol Rovers	0
Half-time:	0-0
Attendance:	4,507
Referee:	Kevin McNally (Hooton)
Halifax Town:	Smith, Burgin, Quinn, Hale, Pickering, Rhodes, Jones, Ford, Kemp, Shanahan, Pugh. Substitute: Wilkie for Ford (71 mins)
Bristol Rovers:	Eadie, Jacobs, Parsons, Green, Taylor, Prince, Rudge, Stanton, Warboys, Bannister, Dobson. Substitute: Fearnley

Alan Warboys returned to the Rovers team, following his hamstring injury, against a Halifax side who had suffered only one home defeat since 27 February 1973. Don Megson switched John Rudge to the right flank to the exclusion of Fearnley, who became substitute. Halifax were without suspended top-scorer David Gwyther as they became the next team attempting to deprive Rovers of their unbeaten League record. The weather was cold and windy but dry, while the pitch was soft but in a reasonable playing condition.

Rovers played into the sun in the first half and it was a cautious start by the leaders, who seemed reluctant to move too far forward into the Halifax half. As Rovers began to settle down, Dobson squared a low pass into the goalmouth where Rudge skied it over the bar with a first-time shot on the turn. Rovers' defence looked frail when Quinn burst past Taylor and charged goalwards, but Jacobs, quick to spot the danger, raced across the penalty area to deflect his shot wide. With Rovers' three forwards interchanging positions regularly, Bannister opened up the home defence with a fine pass to Warboys. His cross from the right looked perfectly flighted for Rudge's head, but a stretching Burgin managed to deflect the ball away.

The sun had sunk down behind the banking and was not a problem to Halifax as it had been to Rovers in the first half. Rovers, striving to find some kind of rhythm, were the first to get a goal attempt in the second half – a long shot by Stanton that was narrowly wide. Eadie's long clearance went deep into Halifax's half, Warboys gave chase and turned the ball to Bannister, who side-footed it inches wide, but was ruled offside anyway. Then, as Halifax's defence shielded a long pass to goalkeeper Smith from Bannister's challenge, Rudge slipped around behind and toed a shot just wide. Ten minutes from the end the game came to life as Halifax forced three corners in quick succession, but the pressure ended with Rudge's long clearance. Just before the end, Dobson put in a rare, on-target shot which Smith gathered safely, and then Bannister hit in a shot on the run which deflected off Pickering's foot into Smith's arms. 'Champ-i-ons, Champ-i-ons!' chanted the vociferous band of Rovers fans during the game at The Shay, but some of the steam had gone out of the Rovers promotion push. However, they continued to measure up to manager Megson's prime demand – that of being a difficult team to beat.

SATURDAY 19 JANUARY 1974, EASTVILLE STADIUM

Bristol Rovers	3 – Warboys, Rudge, Bannister (penalty)
Bournemouth	0
Half-time:	1-0
Attendance:	21,186
Referee:	Ken Burns (Stourbridge)
Bristol Rovers:	Eadie, Jacobs, Parsons, Green, Taylor, Prince, Rudge, Stanton, Warboys, Bannister, Dobson. Substitute: Fearnley
Bournemouth:	Baker, Payne, Howe, Gabriel, Jones, Powell, Redknapp, Cave, Sainty, Boyer, Buttle. Substitute: Miller

With Rovers' lead over second-placed Bournemouth reduced to three points, the meeting of the two clubs at Eastville became particularly critical to both teams' championship hopes. The BBC's *Match of the Day* team also recognised the importance of the game, including it as one of the featured matches broadcast that night. Bournemouth were manager-less by choice since John Bond had joined Norwich City in November 1973; the man with the responsibility for playing affairs at Dean Court was twenty-six-year-old Trevor Hartley. Alan Warboys was passed fit just half-an-hour before the kick-off, so both teams were unchanged for the vital promotion clash. The Eastville pitch, which had not been played on for three weeks, was in good condition considering the amount of rain that had fallen recently. Rovers won the toss and Bournemouth kicked off towards the Tote End, looking intent on taking the fight to Rovers.

Bournemouth's Jimmy Gabriel clears the ball from John Rudge in front of a large Eastville crowd.

Alan Warboys raises his arm after turning the ball over the Bournemouth goal line from John Rudge's cross.

Taylor was forced to concede an early corner, and after Buttle's kick had been pushed out from the goalmouth David Jones volleyed the ball just over Rovers' bar. Rovers first threatened with a burst by Dobson down the left, which ended with a 25yd-drive over the bar, quickly followed by a Parsons cross-shot that went just wide of the far post. The menacing Phil Boyer then had a half-chance, but the Bournemouth forward shot straight at Eadie. Rovers were awarded a free-kick on the halfway line when Tony Powell, Bournemouth's Bristol-born skipper, obstructed Stanton. Warboys jumped high to meet Jacobs' kick and Baker made a smart save. Rovers made the vital breakthrough after 22 minutes when Bannister sent Rudge away down the right and he squeezed his way around Howe, taking the ball almost to the by-line before stroking it into the goalmouth, where it was forced in by Warboys.

Rovers went close to adding a quick second goal when a shot on the turn by Bannister was tipped over by Kieron Baker. Cave's long throws, which had caused problems for Rovers on several occasions in the first half, brought more trouble as he projected the ball into the near post and Taylor was forced to concede a corner. The corner was cleared and Rovers hit back with a swift attack in which Rudge and Bannister conspired to send Warboys through, but his shot on the run was blasted over.

Rovers increased their lead after 55 minutes with a goal by John Rudge – his third in four games since returning. A Warboys shot cannoned off Jimmy Gabriel to Bannister, who pushed the ball across the penalty area to Rudge, who hit a drive which Baker got his hands to but could not stop and the ball spun over the line. Three minutes later Rovers should have sewn up the game when awarded a penalty as Jones brought down Warboys in the box, but Bannister lifted his spot kick over the bar. Bournemouth could have come back into the game when Boyer found an opening, but he clipped his shot wide, while Sainty got the ball in the net but the goal was disallowed because of a foul on Eadie. Ten minutes from the end, Rovers were awarded their second penalty when Bannister stumbled to the ground after a challenge by Gabriel. Bannister atoned for his earlier miss, striking the ball high again but this time it squeezed just under the bar in the corner.

This hard and exciting game provided excellent entertainment for Rovers' second-best League crowd of the season, teamwork being the key to Rovers' success against the Cherries, although Trevor Jacobs, Frankie Prince and John Rudge gave their game an extra lift.

SUNDAY 27 JANUARY 1974, RECREATION GROUND, ALDERSHOT

Aldershot	2 – Brown, Walden
Bristol Rovers	3 – Bannister 2, Warboys
Half-time:	0-0
Attendance:	13,196
Referee:	Jack Taylor (Wolverhampton)
Aldershot:	Johnson, Walden, Walker, Wallace, Dean, Richardson, Walton, Brown, Howarth, Joslyn, Brodie. Substitute: Bell for Wallace (70 mins)
Bristol Rovers:	Eadie, Jacobs, Parsons, Green, Taylor, Prince, Rudge, Stanton, Warboys, Bannister, Dobson. Substitute: Fearnley

Tom Stanton breaks between two Aldershot defenders to shoot for goal during the Sunday League game at the Recreation Ground.

Rovers' game at Aldershot, scheduled for Saturday 26 January, was switched to the following day as Saturday was a 'working day' in Aldershot, one of three consecutive days allocated for fuel consumption under the government's measures to restrict the use of oil during the winter political crisis. The game at Aldershot, Rovers' first Sunday Football League match, added a staggering 8,000 to their average crowd for League matches, and at least 1,000 more fans broke into the ground, which was situated in a public park. Aldershot, the Third Division's revival side with seventeen points out of a possible twenty-two, faced an unchanged Rovers team who had drawn five out of their previous six away games.

Rovers had a setback at the start when centre half Stuart Taylor went off for three stitches to a cut lip received when he was kicked by Aldershot centre forward Jack Howarth. Aldershot were given an early taste of Rovers' striking power when Warboys brought a fingertip save from goalkeeper Glen Johnson following fine work from Bannister and Rudge. Rovers' tremendous desire and ability to win the ball spoiled Aldershot's rhythm in a goalless first half which ended with the home side just having the edge.

Rovers, held by Aldershot for much of the first half, found their form after the interval when Johnson tipped over a 25yd-drive by Bannister, and then in the 49th minute took a deserved lead. A through-ball by Rudge was headed down by Warboys to Bannister and he drove the ball high into the net. Murray Brodie missed a chance for Aldershot, shooting into the side netting, but it was Rovers all the way with Johnson saving spectacularly from Dobson. Bannister completed his double, punishing Aldershot for a bad mistake by captain Len Walker, who allowed Warboys to get past him. The centre forward's shot cannoned off a defender to Bannister, who promptly picked his spot with a perfectly measured low drive. Frankie Prince cashed in on another error by the unfortunate Walker which left Warboys free on the left to score Rovers' third goal after 81 minutes. Uncharacteristically, Rovers relaxed and with 8 minutes to go, a too casual Mike Green backpass was slotted past Jim Eadie by Dennis Brown. Suddenly Aldershot, the most improved side in the division, sensed there was still time to save a point.

Eadie gave the home side further hope when he carried the ball outside his area and conceded a free-kick, from which Richard Walden made the score 3-2 with a clever chip over the defensive wall. But Aldershot went the way of nineteen other clubs who had failed to lower Rovers' colours, and stretched Rovers' unbeaten run to twenty-seven games, equalling a record for a season which they set in the old Third Division South in 1952/53. The win put Rovers seven points clear at the top of the table and left themselves and First Division leaders Leeds United as the only unbeaten teams in the Football League.

29 JANUARY 1974

	P	W	D	L	F	A	Pts
ROVERS	27	15	12	0	49	17	42
Bournemouth	27	14	7	6	34	24	35
York City	25	11	12	2	33	18	34
Chesterfield	27	12	9	6	28	21	33
Huddersfield Town	28	11	9	8	37	33	31
Wrexham	26	12	6	8	35	26	30

SATURDAY 2 FEBRUARY 1974, THE RACECOURSE GROUND, WREXHAM

Wrexham	1 – Griffiths
Bristol Rovers	0
Half-time:	0-0
Attendance:	9,883
Referee:	Walter Johnson (Kendal)
Wrexham:	Lloyd, Jones, Fogg, Evans, May, Whittle, Tinnion, Sutton, Davies, Smallman, Griffiths. Substitute: Ashcroft
Bristol Rovers:	Eadie, Jacobs, Parsons, Green, Taylor, Prince, Stephens, Stanton, Rudge, Bannister, Dobson. Substitute: Fearnley for Stephens (69 mins)

As February kicked-off with a daunting trip to Wrexham, Rovers were not only looking to increase their record-breaking unbeaten run in Division Three – which stood at thirty-two games, carrying on from the previous season – but were also looking to improve on their run of seventeen consecutive away matches without defeat. With only one win in their last five visits to Wrexham's Racecourse Ground, the Pirates faced a Robins side that had just surrendered a five-match winning streak and lay sixth in the table. It seemed that everywhere Rovers played they attracted bumper crowds, probably in the hope of their team being the first to take Rovers' unbeaten record. At Wrexham, the attendance of nearly 10,000 was 4,000 above the Welsh club's average so far that season. Rovers, without Alan Warboys but with Kenny Stephens on the right flank for the first time since November, made a cautious start on a treacherous mud-bound pitch.

Wrexham were momentarily in trouble when Stanton found Dobson with a pass out to the left. The winger's chip into the goalmouth was missed by full-back Joey Jones, and it was fortunate that Evans was covering well and he cleared the danger. Wrexham had a greater share of possession but Rovers were quick to counter-attack and had a chance of taking the lead when Stanton's long through-ball sent Bannister clear. Unfortunately, the striker's shot cannoned off the knees of the advancing Lloyd. Wrexham then mounted a series of attacks, but Rovers broke dangerously with Dobson finding Stephens, who was tackled from behind by Fogg just inside the penalty area and was brought down, but Rovers' strong appeals for a penalty were turned down. Eadie got down well to a shot from Smallman, but could not prevent the ball from rebounding off his chest, but Frankie Prince was there to steer it away from danger.

The second half was only a minute old when Wrexham took the lead, when Whittle sent Tinnion away down Wrexham's right and his centre on the run was met by an unmarked Arfon Griffiths, and he headed cleanly past Eadie. Rovers hit back briefly and Lloyd, whose handling of the greasy ball was faultless, dived full-length to cut out Dobson's cross. Rovers continued to press and a Dobson shot went narrowly wide from a Stanton free-kick. Then Taylor, up for another free-kick, side-footed over the bar from only a few yards out when he had looked certain to equalise.

Kenny Stephens attacks the Wrexham defence at the Racecourse Ground.

Mike Green takes on Wrexham's Arfon Griffiths, who scored the winning goal which ended Rovers' impressive unbeaten run.

Bannister slipped through a gap in the Wrexham defence and rounded the advancing Lloyd, but dragged the ball too wide and sent his shot into the side netting. Five minutes from the end, Bannister got the ball into Wrexham's net after Green's free-kick had been deflected off Wrexham's Micky Evans. At first referee Johnson gave a goal, but then spotted his linesman had signalled for offside. Late in the game a quick low shot from Dobson following a corner hit the base of the post as Rovers' last hopes of preserving their record faded.

So there was no champagne for Rovers as their brilliant League run drowned in the mud of the Racecourse Ground, just one hurdle short of their own twenty-one-year-old Third Division record. It was Rovers' first League defeat in thirty-three games since 31 March 1973.

SUNDAY 17 FEBRUARY 1974, VALE PARK, BURSLEM, STOKE

Port Vale	3 – Williams 2, Leonard
Bristol Rovers	1 – Rudge
Half-time:	0-2
Attendance:	8,505
Referee:	Clive Thomas (Treorchy)
Port Vale:	Boswell, Brodie, Griffiths, Tartt, Harris, Horton, Lacey, Woodward, Williams, Leonard, McLaren. Substitute: Mountford for Williams (51 mins)
Bristol Rovers:	Eadie, Jacobs, Parsons, Green, Taylor, Prince, Stephens, Stanton, Rudge, Bannister, Dobson. Substitute: Fearnley for Eadie (45 mins)

Rovers trained at Eastville on the Saturday morning, watched the Bristol City v. Leeds United FA Cup tie in the afternoon and travelled up to the Potteries in the evening for the first Sunday game played at Port Vale. Manager Don Megson named the same line-up that lost at Wrexham, while Port Vale, who had lost only one of their six games since Roy Sproson took over from Gordon Lee as manager in January, were unchanged for the fifth successive game. Port Vale's goalkeeper Alan Boswell, booked by referee Clive Thomas before the game had even started for marking the goal area, then pulled off a tremendous save to deny Tom Stanton. Port Vale took the lead with a goal by centre forward Ray Williams that the Rovers defence insisted was offside. Kenny Stephens was unlucky with two great efforts on goal, the first a magnificent shot that cannoned off the underside of the

crossbar, followed by another that was headed off the goal line by Colin Tartt with Boswell beaten. The next incident changed the course of the game when Jim Eadie was injured in a fearsome collision with Vale's John Woodward. Mike Green took over the goalkeeper's jersey for 3 minutes while Eadie was treated, after being brought round by Rovers' trainer Bobby Campbell beside the side of the goal.

The goalkeeper came back to finish the half, but was obviously not in a fit state to play, and while the big Scotsman was in a state of concussion he allowed the ball to rebound off his chest to present Williams with his second goal. Eadie didn't know the half-time whistle had blown and Green had to lead him to the dressing room. The Rovers' captain made the decision himself to take over the jersey, despite having no experience between the posts. His inexperience was demonstrated 4 minutes into the second half when Rovers stand-in goalkeeper allowed a simple Keith Leonard shot through his legs for Vale's third goal. Rovers fought hard enough, pulled a goal back through

Trainer-coach Bobby Campbell helps a concussed Jim Eadie take off his jersey, watched by referee Clive Thomas and stand-in goalkeeper Mike Green.

Bruce Bannister tries an overhead kick at Port Vale, forming a balletic pose with Vale goalkeeper Alan Boswell.

John Rudge, and for the final 20 minutes showed a crowd double Vale's normal attendance why they were top of the division, but it was too much lost ground to reclaim.

A second-half booking for Frankie Prince for a foul on Woodward, his third of the season, took him to ten points, two points short of the twelve-mark suspension limit. Jim Eadie was taken to hospital, bleeding slightly from his left ear, for an X-ray, but thankfully there was no serious harm and he was back in training three days after his injury.

SATURDAY 23 FEBRUARY 1974, EASTVILLE STADIUM

Bristol Rovers	1 – Warboys
Watford	0
Half-time:	0-0
Attendance:	14,069
Referee:	Harry Powell (Stourport)
Bristol Rovers:	Eadie, Jacobs, Parsons, Green, Taylor, Prince, Stephens, Stanton, Warboys, Bannister, Dobson. Substitute: Rudge for Dobson (45 mins)
Watford:	Rankin, Butler, Williams, Craker, Markham, Keen, Farley, Bond, Jenkins, Scullion, Jennings. Substitute: Welbourne

Don Megson recalled Alan Warboys to lead the attack after watching him come through his final fitness test, springing a surprise by axing John Rudge to make way for the twenty-three-goal striker. It ended a run of seven games for Rudge, who was operating on the right flank before being switched to centre forward when Warboys was injured. Kenny Stephens kept his right-wing role and with Warboys back, the manager wanted to play with two orthodox wingers against in-form promotion outsiders Watford, who had lost only one of their last seven games.

Rovers, playing towards the Tote End, went straight on the attack. Warboys nodded down a Stephens' cross to Bannister, but his co-striker miskicked and sent the ball tamely wide. Mike Keen, Watford's player-manager, was penalised for a foul from behind on Bannister just outside the penalty area. An elaborate free-kick routine took the ball from Dobson to Bannister, but a squared pass into Warboys' path was intercepted. The recalled striker then sent in a flying header but Rankin was positioned on the near post to beat the ball down, and Dobson found Warboys' head again with another left-wing cross, and the ball was nodded to Bannister but his overhead kick was wide of the target.

Alan Warboys scores the match-winning goal in the last minute against Watford. Stuart Taylor, who provided the pass, is in the centre.

Watford hit back with a Farley run but his pass through to Bill Jennings caught the twenty-two-goal striker offside. Stephens was narrowly wide with a shot following a Dobson free-kick and a close-range shot by Bannister was blocked by Butler. Lindsay Parsons, making his 201st consecutive appearance for Rovers, was lectured by the referee for body-checking Stewart Scullion. Rovers went close to taking the lead 5 minutes before half-time when Bannister spurted past Keen and stabbed through a pass to Warboys. The centre forward drove the ball on with a first-time shot which Rankin turned around for a corner.

Dobson, who had limped slightly in the later stages of the first half, suffering trouble from his old foot injury, did not appear after the interval and was replaced by Rudge, who took up his role on the left. Rovers forced two corners, both of which were cleared, and then Frankie Prince, the driving force behind Rovers' attacks, burst through on his own down the left and his shot on the turn was deflected for another corner by Markham. Rovers were unlucky not to take the lead when a Rudge pass sent Warboys through, but his shot was booted off the line by Butler with Rankin beaten. The ball spun out to Bannister, who sent it back with a diving header which again was deflected for a corner. Just when it seemed as if Rovers would have to settle for a point, they snatched victory with a Warboys goal a minute from the end following a free-kick by Jacobs, awarded for a foul on Stanton by Farley. In the dying seconds, Watford almost snatched an equaliser when Jenkins headed inches wide from Dennis Bond's free-kick.

Trainer Bobby Campbell's shouted instructions had played a vital part in securing both points for Rovers when he ordered Alan Warboys back to the middle of the attack after he had begun to feel his hamstring injury and wanted to switch to the wing. He also sent Stuart Taylor into Watford's goalmouth, where his touch from Trevor Jacobs' last-minute free-kick provided Warboys with his twenty-fourth – and final – goal of the season.

27 FEBRUARY 1974

	P	W	D	L	F	A	Pts
ROVERS	30	16	12	2	51	21	44
York City	29	13	13	3	40	22	39
Chesterfield	31	14	10	7	35	26	38
Bournemouth	31	15	8	8	36	29	38
Oldham Athletic	27	14	8	5	41	27	36
Wrexham	30	14	7	9	39	29	35

SATURDAY 2 MARCH 1974, HOME PARK, PLYMOUTH

Plymouth Argyle	1 – Provan
Bristol Rovers	0
Half-time:	0-0
Attendance:	11,374
Referee:	Ron Challis (Tonbridge)
Plymouth Argyle:	Furnell, Randell, Sullivan, Hore, Provan, Saxton, Read, Davey, Mariner, Machin, Darke. Substitute: Rogers
Bristol Rovers:	Eadie, Jacobs, Parsons, Green, Taylor, Prince, Stephens, Stanton, Fearnley, Bannister, Jones. Substitute: Aitken for Prince (60 mins)

Plymouth, unbeaten in their last five League games, had had recent success in the League Cup, finally being beaten 3-1 in January by First Division Manchester City in a two-legged semi-final. Rovers remained secretive about their team plans to the very last minute and when they took the field were without Warboys, Dobson and Rudge. Fearnley took over the No. 9 shirt and Bryn Jones replaced Dobson, who was absent for the first time. It was Jones' fourth first-team appearance of the season and was being brought in as a midfield player in a 4-3-3 formation. A considerable amount of morning rain left the Home Park pitch heavy and holding surface water.

The rain was still falling steadily when the game began. The home team soon settled down and as Rovers came under pressure for the first time, Prince brought down Reed from behind. Green headed away from the resulting free-kick and the ball flew to Darke, whose shot flew over the bar. Rovers' front three constantly switched positions but made little impression on Argyle's defence, and when Bryn Jones found Fearnley with a pass down the left the striker's angled shot was saved comfortably by Furnell. Bannister cleverly left a Jones throw for Stephens, who sent over a fine centre which Saxton intercepted at the expense of a corner.

Argyle went close to taking the lead after 32 minutes when Paul Mariner centred and Davey was unlucky with a neatly flicked header that grazed the bar and landed on the roof of the net. Two minutes later Rovers had a good chance when Fearnley played the ball to Bannister and was put through by a headed return pass, but Furnell was quick off his line and blocked Fearnley's shot. Conditions were becoming farcical and the centre circle had become a skating rink, but just before half-time the sun came out.

Several players changed their mud-coated strips at half-time and Prince appeared with a numberless shirt, which the referee noted in his book. The atrocious conditions ruled out

Kenny Stephens shoots for goal in the rain at Plymouth Argyle.

Tom Stanton shows determination to get past a Plymouth defender.

anything more skilled than kick-and-hope, and it was Plymouth who made the breakthrough after 54 minutes with a goal by Provan. Davey's driven centre from the right was headed wide of the far post by Mike Green as Mariner moved in, but it was only a temporary escape. Reed took the resulting corner and the ball was flicked past Eadie off Davey's head. Plymouth went close to increasing their lead when Eadie mishit a goal-kick and sent it straight to Davey, who was just off-target with a chipped effort.

Right on the hour, Frankie Prince was taken off suffering with flu and teenager Peter Aitken came on for his first taste of League football of the season. Jim Furnell, the former Arsenal goalkeeper, then made another fine save to deny Rovers a share of the points. Argyle conceded a free-kick just outside their penalty area and Green's well-hit shot beat the wall, but Furnell pushed the ball over the bar. Jones' flag kick was forced in by Fearnley with a diving header, but the goal was disallowed for a foul on the goalkeeper.

Despite the loss of three of their last four matches, manager Don Megson believed there was no cause for immediate alarm. Worrying though the recent run of results was, the fact was that Rovers, weakened as they were, still performed well enough to deserve a draw.

TUESDAY 5 MARCH 1974, EASTVILLE STADIUM

Bristol Rovers	1 – Bannister
Rochdale	1 – Bebbington
Half-time:	1-1
Attendance:	11,195
Referee:	Ray Toseland (Kettering)
Bristol Rovers:	Eadie, Jacobs, Parsons, Green, Taylor, Coombes, Stephens, Stanton, Fearnley, Bannister, Dobson. Substitute: Aitken
Rochdale:	Poole, Smith, Seddon, Arnold, Hanvey, Horne, Downes, Taylor, Brennan, Bebbington, Buckley. Substitute: Gowans for Seddon (48 mins)

Jeff Coombes, the nineteen-year-old former Welsh youth cap, was called up in Rovers' midfield to replace the flu-stricken Frankie Prince as floodlit football returned to Eastville, some four months after the government's banning of their use at sporting events. Rovers were also without Warboys who, it was considered, was still not ready for another comeback, and John Rudge was out with an ankle injury. Bottom of the table Rochdale, with only two wins and ten draws to their credit all season, were fourteen points from safety.

However Rochdale, looking odds-on to be relegated from the Third Division, rocked Rovers by taking the lead after only 13 minutes. Bobby Downes' corner was punched out by goalkeeper

Kenny Stephens makes a powerful
challenge on Rochdale centre half Keith
Hanvey.

Bruce Bannister forces his way in front of a Rochdale
defender to head Rovers' equalising goal after 30
minutes.

Jim Eadie, but the ball was played back in by Steve Arnold to Keith Bebbington, whose shot was
blocked by Stuart Taylor. Bebbington moved in and measured a great drive from the edge of the
penalty area, the ball soaring high into the net.

A shot by Kenny Stephens hit goalkeeper Mike Poole and the ball rolled away for a corner, and
then full-back Seddon headed off the line from Bannister. Poole then had to dive spectacularly
to hold a powerful 25yd-shot from Tom Stanton. Rovers equalised on the half-hour when Gordon
Fearnley robbed full-back Smith, shook off a challenge and broke through on the left. He rounded
off his great run with a centre to the far post where Bannister forced his way between two Rochdale
defenders to head his fourteenth goal of the season.

Trevor Jacobs, safe in defence, also displayed an attractive flair for attack, linking well with
Stephens and Bannister, and Rochdale survived more by luck than judgement until half-time. The
second half saw Rovers continue to press with Jeff Coombes, in his first senior game of the season,
who showed good imagination with his use of the ball from the midfield. Bannister headed the ball
onto the bar and Rovers might have had a penalty when Bebbington upended Stephens well inside
the penalty area. Mike Green had two good chances from corner kicks, one header dropped a yard
wide and he missed another by scooping the ball high over the bar from 4yds out. Rovers' last
chance went with a well-taken shot on the run by Stephens, which beat goalkeeper Poole but the
ball rolled a foot wide. Despite their many team changes Rovers still looked in a better class, but
Rochdale, despite glaring weaknesses, made up the difference with a spirited challenge.

FRIDAY 8 MARCH 1974, EASTVILLE STADIUM

Bristol Rovers	2 – Bannister, John (M)
Huddersfield Town	1 – Gowling
Half-time:	2-0
Attendance:	13,543
Referee:	Bert Newsome (Codsall)
Bristol Rovers:	Eadie, Jacobs, Aitken, Green, Taylor, Prince, Stephens, Stanton, Staniforth, Bannister, John (M). Substitute: Fearnley
Huddersfield Town:	Poole, Hutt, Garner, Smith, Saunders, Dolan, Hoy, Lawson, Gowling, Pugh, Summerill. Substitute: Grey for Hoy (65 mins)

Bruce Bannister stabs in the first goal against Huddersfield into the roof of the net, with defenders Poole and Garner motionless.

Malcolm John celebrates his first full game of the season by sliding the ball over the line for what proved to be the winning goal against Huddersfield.

Huddersfield Town and their manager, Ian Greaves, had halted the slide which took them from Division One to the Third Division in two seasons, and were on the fringe of the promotion challengers. However, they had only won two of their seventeen away fixtures. Lindsay Parsons' great run for Rovers – 203 consecutive first team appearances – ended one game earlier than expected for the consistent full-back, who was due to start a two-match suspension the following Tuesday; he had a groin strain. New signing Dave Staniforth, leading the attack, worked on linking up with co-striker Bruce Bannister when he trained with his new colleagues for the first time on the morning of the game, and Malcolm John was selected for his first full League game for two years. The match was played on the Friday night to avoid a clash with Saturday's FA Cup quarter-final at Ashton Gate, where Bristol City met League champions Liverpool.

Rovers were soon on the lookout for goals and a Stuart Taylor header was nodded off the line by full-back Paul Garner, and when Terry Poole dived to save from Kenny Stephens, Huddersfield centre half John Saunders booted the ball clear. Poole then brought off a double-fisted save when Staniforth who, after linking up with Bannister, blasted in a great drive from just outside the penalty area. The goal which always seemed likely materialised in the 18th minute, when Malcolm John flighted a corner from the left to Stephens who drove the ball hard and low into the centre of the goalmouth where Bannister side-footed it into the net.

Huddersfield kept possession well, working the ball attractively upfield, but were unable to find a way through a quick-covering Rovers defence. Rovers increased their lead with a goal from twenty-two-year-old Welshman Malcolm John, continuing where he left off in April 1972 when he scored the only goal of the game at home to Halifax Town. Tom Stanton seized on a mistake by Stephen Smith and sent Stephens racing away on the right and once again his hard, low cross into the middle was prodded into the net, this time by Malcolm John at the second attempt. Poole got his hand to the first shot, but failed to hold the ball and John followed up to score.

In a rare chance for the Terriers, goalkeeper Jim Eadie beat out an angled drive from Gowling, the only forward to threaten Rovers, early in the second half. Trevor Jacobs came nearest to adding to Rovers' score with a left-footed 25yd-shot which glanced behind off a post. Three minutes from the end Alan Gowling lobbed the ball over first Mike Green and then Stuart Taylor before smashing it past Jim Eadie with his left foot from just outside the penalty area. It was the former Manchester United striker's twentieth goal of the season.

Despite the narrow margin of the victory, Rovers were never in danger of dropping a point in a game that attracted a bevy of managers, including Bertie Mee of Arsenal, Bill Shankly of Liverpool, Ted Bates of Southampton and Portsmouth boss John Mortimore.

TUESDAY 12 MARCH 1974, EASTVILLE STADIUM

Bristol Rovers	3 – Jacobs (2), Bannister
Blackburn Rovers	0
Half-time:	2-0
Attendance:	14,029
Referee:	Malcolm Sinclair (Guildford)
Bristol Rovers:	Eadie, Jacobs, Aitken, Green, Taylor, Prince, Stephens, Stanton, Staniforth, Bannister, John (M). Substitute: Fearnley
Blackburn Rovers:	Bradshaw, Heaton, Hutchins, Martin, Waddington, Fazackerley, Napier, Metcalfe, Endean, Parkes, Field. Substitute: Arentoft

In the previous season, Blackburn had failed by just two points to return to the Second Division. Being within striking distance of the leading clubs at the time of their visit to Eastville, they were looking for a run of wins to put themselves back in the promotion race. The return of Barry Endean and Stuart Metcalfe made Blackburn's line-up the strongest they had fielded since the start of the year; Don Megson was happy to name an unchanged team after Friday's return to championship form.

Blackburn's seventeen-year-old England youth goalkeeper Paul Bradshaw (who joined the Pirates thirteen years later) came under fire immediately against the slick-moving Rovers side. After making a spectacular save from Kenny Stephens, Bradshaw was beaten in the 10th minute by Trevor Jacobs' second goal of the season. The Rovers full-back ran on superbly down the right to latch on to a raking 40yd-pass from Stuart Taylor, and as Bradshaw hurried across to the near post Jacobs beat him with an acutely angled low drive. The ball skidded between the goalkeeper

and the post and bounced into the net off the opposite post. Kit Napier should have equalised after 19 minutes when Heaton put Metcalfe clear and his hard-hit centre pierced Rovers' defence, but from only 3yds out Napier scooped the ball high over an empty net. Blackburn paid for this miss when Jacobs struck again after 30 minutes, again aided by Stuart Taylor.

The Rovers centre half pounced on a clearance from John Waddington and pushed the ball to Jacobs, who hammered in a high left-footed shot and the ball slipped off the up-stretched hands of Bradshaw and

Above: Trevor Jacobs' long-range shot beats Bradshaw for his, and Rovers', second goal against Blackburn Rovers.

Below: Blackburn's goalkeeper Paul Bradshaw safely gathers a cross intended for the head of Bruce Bannister.

found the net just under the bar to put Rovers two goals up. Bradshaw had no respite and in the 38th minute made another stop from Kenny Stephens. The Rovers winger had the ball in the net for a third time, but referee Malcolm Sinclair refused to allow the goal because he said that he had signalled for half-time a split-second before Stephens had shot. Blackburn's defence came under further pressure in the second half with Don Martin blocking a shot from Stephens, and Bannister drove a yard wide from the edge of the area. In a rare raid by Blackburn, goalkeeper Jim Eadie dived at full stretch to make his first save of the game from Endean.

Rovers should have had a penalty when Dave Staniforth was brought down from behind by John Waddington after latching on to Don Hutchins' backpass. A great Stephens shot was blocked by Martin, a disallowed Staniforth goal after a narrow offside decision and a Trevor Jacobs shot that went inches wide, denying him a hat-trick, all happened before Blackburn's fate was sealed with 11 minutes remaining. Bannister was the victim of a foul by Heaton that earned Rovers a free-kick just 10yds out from the Blackburn goal line. With every visiting player strung across the goal, Tom Stanton touched the free-kick to Bannister, who lashed the ball in under the bar. With York City losing 2-1 against Oldham Athletic that same evening, Rovers reopened a five-point lead at the top of the table. Oldham, with three games in hand, were now the main danger to Rovers' title hopes.

13 MARCH 1974

	P	W	D	L	F	A	Pts
ROVERS	34	18	13	3	57	24	49
York City	33	15	14	4	47	26	44
Oldham Athletic	31	18	8	5	52	30	44
Chesterfield	35	16	11	8	42	30	43
Bournemouth	34	16	9	9	41	36	41
Wrexham	32	15	8	9	41	30	38

SATURDAY 16 MARCH 1974, BOOTHAM CRESCENT, YORK

York City	2 – Jones, Holmes (penalty)
Bristol Rovers	1 – Stephens
Half-time:	0-0
Attendance:	10,330
Referee:	Jim Whalley (Southport)
York City:	Crawford, Stone, Burrows, Holmes, Swallow, Topping, Lyons, Calvert, Seal, Jones, Woodward. Substitute: Pollard
Bristol Rovers:	Eadie, Jacobs, Aitken, Green, Taylor, Prince, Stephens, Stanton, Staniforth, Bannister, Dobson. Substitute: Rudge for Staniforth (77 mins)

Malcolm John, who played in the last two home League games and scored against Huddersfield, made an eve-of-transfer-deadline move to Northampton Town on Thursday 14 March, teaming up with Bill Dodgin junior and John Petts, the former Eastville favourite, on loan for the remainder

Graeme Crawford dives headlong at the feet of Dave Staniforth during Rovers' top of the table clash at York, with Bannister in attendance.

Stuart Taylor moves up for a powerful header at a corner, with Dave Staniforth lending support.

of the season. Don Megson decided against playing Gerry O'Brien, his new loan signing from Southampton, because of his unfamiliarity with the team's play, so Rovers showed just one change, with Colin Dobson returning to the left wing in place of Malcolm John.

Rovers, top of the division, and York, chasing them hard in second place, kicked off in blustery conditions at a tightly packed stadium, the crowd boosted by a big Rovers following. Both clubs usually boasted a prolific strikeforce, and it was the home pair who first threatened when Chris Jones shot wide before Jimmy Seal also headed narrowly over the bar. Rovers 'keeper Jim Eadie then kept out the dangerous Jones, while winger Kenny Stephens was a regular menace at the opposite end as he attempted to pick out the lively Bruce Bannister, who was on this occasion lacking his regular partner Alan Warboys.

However, defences continued to rule as the first half remained scoreless. York had an escape early in the second period as right-back John Stone headed off the line, with Crawford well beaten, from a Colin Dobson shot following a Tom Stanton free-kick. And that looked even more vital when the home side took the lead on 52 minutes. Ian Holmes set off on a thrusting run down the left and beat three Rovers defenders before crossing low for Jones to crash the ball into the roof of the net from close range. But the visitors had been the division's outstanding side all season, and responded with Frank Prince having a 25yd-effort well saved by Graeme Crawford. Dave Staniforth then broke clear before being thwarted by a tremendous last-ditch challenge from Phil Burrows. The resolute Stone also blocked from Staniforth and play soon went back up towards the opposite end for Holmes to rattle the woodwork. The game then erupted on 81 minutes when Rovers' striker Bannister was sent off for elbowing Chris Topping in the mouth after being fouled by the defender, who was booked.

But even with ten men Rovers rallied and levelled with just 5 minutes left when Kenny Stephens' wind-assisted shot sneaked inside the far post to the delight of the travelling fans. However, York weren't finished and right-winger Barry Lyons forced a great save from Eadie before his side dramatically snatched a winner in the 5th minute of injury time. After a corner was delivered, home midfielder John Woodward was knocked to the ground and a penalty awarded. The visitors were incensed and the already cautioned Kenny Stephens was dismissed for arguing with the referee over the penalty. It was left to Holmes to decide the contest with the last kick of the game, and he calmly slotted home from the spot to spark wild celebrations on the terraces from the home faithful.

Two Rovers men were sent off and four more booked, as well as two York players, in a sensational top-of-the-table-clash that was hard fought, but never a dirty game.

TUESDAY 19 MARCH 1974, EASTVILLE STADIUM

Bristol Rovers	1 – Staniforth
Wrexham	0
Half-time:	0-0
Attendance:	14,510
Referee:	Jim Bent (Hemel Hempstead)
Bristol Rovers:	Eadie, Jacobs, Aitken, Green, Taylor, Prince, Stephens, Stanton, Staniforth, Bannister, O'Brien. Substitute: Fearnley
Wrexham:	Lloyd, Jones, Fogg, Evans, May, Whittle, Tinnion, Sutton, Ashcroft, Davies, Griffiths. Substitute: Davis for Davies (80 mins)

Match winner Dave Staniforth
threatens the Wrexham defence under
the Eastville floodlights.

Bruce Bannister sends a shot inches
past the Wrexham post.

Wrexham's FA Cup exploits had tended to overshadow their Third Division performances, but they were handily placed behind the leading clubs as the season neared its final month. Their fine FA Cup run ended at Burnley in the sixth round, and it was, of course, Wrexham who ended Rovers twenty-seven-game unbeaten run with a 1-0 win at the Racecourse Ground on 2 February. Wrexham were without their Welsh Under-23 striker, David Smallman, and Micky Thomas, who would have deputised, was also injured. Gerry O'Brien, Rovers' £40,000-rated loan signing from Southampton, was selected having trained the previous Friday and watched the controversial clash with York on Saturday. Most of the early excitement surrounded O'Brien's debut and the skilful Scot did not disappoint, his ball skills and speed down both flanks made him an instant hit with the big Eastville crowd. With Kenny Stephens doing likewise, chances were being carved out but the punch was missing in front of goal.

The first clear chance of the game fell to Bannister after 15 minutes when Peter Aitken's cross found him clear 12yds out, but the Rovers striker twisted himself badly as he shot and, after goalkeeper Brian Lloyd collected easily, he needed attention from the trainer. It was Bannister who had the next chance too, when he headed inches wide from a loose backpass by Griffiths. In the 25th minute Mel Sutton, the star of Wrexham's cultured middle line, split Rovers' defence with a finely judged pass. Geoff Davies latched on to it and got past Jim Eadie, but as he moved to finish off the attack he was impeded by Trevor Jacobs. It gave Stuart Taylor that moment's respite which Rovers needed, and he thumped the ball behind. The awarding of a corner instead of a penalty so upset player-coach Arfon Griffiths that he was booked for dissent.

After 31 minutes, Sutton, clean through, was dragged back by the shirt-sleeve by Peter Aitken for a free-kick that came to nothing, and 8 minutes later Graham Whittle clipped the ball home after Davies had headed down Brian Tinnion's right-wing cross – only to have the goal disallowed for offside. The Welshmen's high-speed breaks out of defence were continually catching out the Rovers defence and it needed all of goalkeeper Eadie's concentration to keep the scoreline blank, but the next narrow escape was at the Wrexham goal when Staniforth's clever back-heel was scooped off the line by Joey Jones.

Ten minutes from time, Dave Staniforth, the £20,000 signing from Sheffield United, scored a crucial first goal for his new club. Frankie Price took a throw-in which found Bannister out on the left. Bannister's quick through-ball was met by Staniforth, who turned in a flash and rifled a powerful left-footed shot just inside the near post under Brian Lloyd's crossbar from the narrowest of angles. Outclassed and outplayed for most of the match, it was a win Rovers badly needed after the York setback, on a night when menacing rivals Oldham beat Bournemouth 4-2.

SATURDAY 23 MARCH 1974, EASTVILLE STADIUM

Bristol Rovers	0
Walsall	2 – Buckley (2, 1 penalty)
Half-time:	0-1
Attendance:	11,370
Referee:	Anthony Oliver (Leigh-on-Sea)
Bristol Rovers:	Eadie, Jacobs, Parsons, Green, Taylor, Prince, Stephens, Stanton, Staniforth, Bannister, Dobson. Substitute: Rudge for Staniforth (65 mins)
Walsall:	Kearns, Saunders, Fry, Robinson, Bennett, Atthey, Sloan, Taylor, Andrews, Buckley, Harrison. Substitute: Wright for Bennett (49 mins)

Walsall, who had been in the Third Division since leaving Division Two at the end of the 1962/63 season, had soldiered on manager-less since Ronnie Allen and his assistant, Bristol-born David Burnside, left in December for economic reasons. Acting manager Doug Fraser named himself in the squad of a much-improved Walsall side positioned in ninth place in the League. Rovers' loan signing Gerry O'Brien was axed after only one appearance, but Don Megson stressed that the skilful Scot had been sacrificed for the sake of the balance of the team, and not because the manager was dissatisfied with his individual performance on his debut against Wrexham.

Rovers, a stiff breeze in their backs, kicked off towards the Tote End in the first half of a game played on a firm pitch, and moved quickly into attack. Kearns, Walsall's goalkeeper, was forced to move smartly as Dobson moved in on the far post towards a looping Jacobs cross from the right. But Walsall, in an all-red strip, soon settled down and impressed as a busy, workmanlike side. Rovers, badly needing a good performance to bolster their sagging confidence, were shaken in the 19th minute when Walsall took a surprise lead. Harrison pushed the ball down the left to

Midfield man Tom Stanton is tackled by two Walsall defenders as he tries to cross the ball.

Brian Taylor, whose gentle lob into the goalmouth found Alan Buckley on his own. He flicked the ball forwards with his head, beating Eadie with a perfectly placed attempt to the goalkeeper's left, for his twenty-first goal of the season. Rovers were stung into immediate retaliation when Kenny Stephens, looking sharp against his former club, was brought down by a wild tackle from full-back Fry, for which he was booked.

Rovers' final attempt to draw level before the end of a poor first-half performance came after Bannister had been fouled from behind by Saunders. Dobson's free-kick was headed out by Robinson, but straight to Stuart Taylor, whose first time shot flashed narrowly wide. Four minutes after the restart, Rovers went close to equalising when Kearns failed to hold a Stanton cross. In the goalmouth scramble that followed, Staniforth got his foot to the ball first but Kearns recovered well to push the centre forward's shot around the post for a corner. Walsall's centre half Bennett was injured in the mêlée and was eventually carried off on a stretcher. Play was held up for 4 minutes by the incident and when it eventually restarted, Stephens's corner was headed just over the bar by Staniforth. Then, after 61 minutes, another incredible lapse in Rovers' defence resulted in a Walsall penalty. Substitute Wright ran past five Rovers' men in a 30yd-run before scooping the ball over to Andrews, who headed the ball goalwards. Eadie was stranded out of goal and Mike Green pushed the ball around the post with both hands and was lucky to escape a booking. Buckley collected his second goal of the game as he hit the penalty cleanly past Eadie.

As Rovers made desperate late efforts to get back in the game, Harrison cleared off the line from Prince and Kearns did well to push a volley by substitute Rudge over the bar. Suddenly, the Third Division leaders, who had looked certain to win the championship for so long, were vulnerable, crashing to their first home defeat of the season by a middle-of-table side. It was Rovers' fifth loss in their last ten games, with only two points from their last three matches.

Mike Green, Frankie Prince and Colin Dobson in pensive mood during a pause in the 2-0 home defeat against Walsall.

MONDAY 25 MARCH 1974, SPOTLAND, ROCHDALE

Rochdale	0
Bristol Rovers	1 – Bannister
Half-time:	0-0
Attendance:	1,499
Referee:	Vince James (York)
Rochdale:	Poole, Bradbury, Hanvey, Horne, Arnold, Marsh, Bebbington, Gowans, Brennan, Carrick, Downes. Substitute: Tobin
Bristol Rovers:	Eadie, Jacobs, Parsons, Green, Taylor, Prince, O'Brien, Stanton, Rudge, Bannister, Stephens. Substitute: Warboys for O'Brien (78 mins)

Rovers travelled north on the Sunday and trained on Huddersfield Town's ground on the morning of the match against bottom club Rochdale; the Rovers party included loan signing Gerry O'Brien, who was left out of the previous Saturday's team, and Bryn Jones. Don Megson named Alan Warboys as substitute, planning to break him back into football gently after six weeks on the injured list with hamstring trouble. The manager, thinking about the following Saturday's vital top-of-the-table clash at Chesterfield, feared another false start by his star striker and Warboys was expected to play in only the final half-hour at Spotland. Megson shook up his attack, dropping Dave Staniforth and Colin Dobson, with John Rudge spearheading the attack, Kenny Stephens switching from the right to the left wing, and Gerry O'Brien taking over on the right.

Rovers' goal, after only 14 minutes, was an absolute gift by the home side. Goalkeeper Mick Poole tapped a goal-kick to left-back Keith Hanvey, who was on the edge of the Rochdale penalty area. Hanvey stroked the ball back, but an alert John Rudge got to it before Poole and rolled it across the goalmouth to give Bannister what must have been the simplest chance of his career. All he had to do was tap the ball into the empty net for his fifteenth League goal of the season.

A cleverly worked offside trap kept Rochdale in check and a weak drive by Bobby Downes was all Jim Eadie had to deal with in the opening half. Gerry O'Brien had a great chance to add to Rovers' lead after 33 minutes, but his measured shot from the right of the goal was fisted away by Poole. Rudge then sent one shot into the side netting and had another brilliantly held by the goalkeeper.

Rochdale made a spirited start to the second half with Jim Eadie saving a header by Mike Brennan, but scoring chances were few and far between. Neither O'Brien nor Kenny Stephens could make much progress on either wing, with the result that Rovers created few chances. Rudge tried to bring the game to life and a splendidly struck right-footed drive in the 69th minute was pushed aside by Poole as he dived at full stretch. Alan Warboys came on 12 minutes from the end in the place of O'Brien and soon made his presence felt when he broke through the middle onto a defence-splitting pass from Frankie Prince. The striker caught the ball perfectly on the run and fired in a terrific drive which Poole failed to hold, but managed to pounce on and clear.

Jimmy Frizzell, manager of Rovers' arch-rivals Oldham, and most of his team were at the match to size up the form of their opposition in the race for the title, but there was little to be gleaned from a Rovers performance that failed to add the finishing touches to often-incisive approach work. But the result was all that mattered to Rovers.

SATURDAY 30 MARCH 1974, SALTERGATE, CHESTERFIELD

Chesterfield	0
Bristol Rovers	0
Half-time:	0-0
Attendance:	11,559
Referee:	Peter Willis (Meadowfield)
Chesterfield:	Tingay, Holmes, Burton, McHale, Winstanley, Barlow, Phelan, Moss, Kowalski, Bellamy, Wilson. Substitute: Stott
Bristol Rovers:	Eadie, Jacobs, Parsons, Green, Taylor, Prince, Stephens, Stanton, Rudge, Bannister, Dobson. Substitute: Staniforth for Bannister (79 mins)

The news from Eastville on the Friday prior to the promotion clash with Chesterfield was that Alan Warboys needed to rest for another fortnight, following a visit to London to see Arsenal's consultant specialist. The specialist's diagnosis of Warboys' hamstring injury was the same as that of Rovers' own medical staff – that its recurrence was caused by the breakdown of scar tissue. Fourth-placed Chesterfield had recently ended Oldham's run of ten successive victories with a 1-0 win at Saltergate, but were considered promotion outsiders by their manager Joe Shaw. With Chesterfield playing in blue, Rovers wore their black-and-white change strip as they played into a hazy sun on a warm afternoon.

The League leaders soon put pressure on Chesterfield's goal and forced a corner in a raid down the right led by Bannister. Stephens' kick was headed behind the far post by Phelan for another corner. This time Dobson's cross was cleared cleanly. Chesterfield, with Moss and Kowalski looking menacing down the middle, had a Wilson shot hammered into the side netting, and then a slip by Stuart Taylor almost cost Rovers a goal. The centre half was caught in possession and as he tried to control a pass back to him from Dobson, he slipped and Moss moved clear. But Eadie came to Rovers' rescue with a quick challenge on the Chesterfield striker and managed to deflect the low shot with his legs. Then Eadie was pulled up for taking too many steps while carrying the ball to the edge of the penalty area. In his disgust over the ruling, the goalkeeper booted the ball into the crowd and earned himself a booking. The free-kick was rolled to McHale, whose shot was blocked by Rovers' wall. Rovers almost snatched the lead with a great shot by Bannister, who moved down the right on to a good through-ball from Stanton, but his shot from an acute angle was pushed around the near post by a diving Tingay.

Just before half-time, Trevor Jacobs took a free-kick which was partially cleared, and Chesterfield were fortunate to block a ferocious drive by Stanton from the edge of the penalty area. Rovers came out fast after the interval, but two promising moves were halted when strikers Rudge and Bannister were caught in Chesterfield's offside trap. Rovers had a chance of going ahead when Bannister pulled back a low centre to Prince, who had a clear shot at goal from the edge of the penalty area, but the midfield man hit his low shot a couple of yards wide. Chesterfield responded with a series of fast raids, but they never really carried enough power to threaten Rovers' defence.

Rovers again went close to taking the lead when Stephens drove over a dangerous centre which Winstanley almost turned into his own net. Winstanley then went desperately close to breaking the deadlock in the closing minutes, but Rovers had mastered Chesterfield's attack well before the end. Manager Don Megson, facing the toughest test of his career during the leaders' alarming slump in form, reacted by reverting to a 4-4-2 formation which enabled Rovers to stop Chesterfield's midfield section from functioning effectively and still left Rudge and Bannister able to put pressure on the home defence. With their lead cut to three points – closest rivals York and Oldham both picked up a point on the leaders with impressive victories over Brighton and Shrewsbury respectively – Megson warned, 'It's back to the basics for us. At the start of the season we were a hard side to beat, and that's how it's going to be from now on'.

Bruce Bannister tries to force his way through the Chesterfield defence, with Frankie Prince on the right.

30 MARCH 1974

	P	W	D	L	F	A	Pts
ROVERS	39	20	14	5	60	28	54
York City	37	18	15	4	58	31	51
Oldham Athletic	36	20	9	7	60	38	49
Chesterfield	39	18	13	8	47	33	49
Wrexham	37	18	9	10	49	33	45
Bournemouth	38	16	10	12	49	49	42

TUESDAY 2 APRIL 1974, EASTVILLE STADIUM

Bristol Rovers	2 – Staniforth, Rudge
Aldershot	1 – Walton
Half-time:	1-0
Attendance:	12,746
Referee:	Ken Baker (Rugby)
Bristol Rovers:	Eadie, Jacobs, Parsons, Green, Taylor, Prince, Stephens, Stanton, Rudge, Staniforth, Dobson. Substitute: O'Brien
Aldershot:	Johnson, Walden, Jopling, Walker, Dean, Richardson, Walton, Brown, Howarth, Joslyn, Brodie. Substitute: Stenson for Walker (60 mins)

Aldershot, promoted for the first time ever the previous season, came to Eastville with an unbeaten run of six games behind them as the promotion run-in really got underway. Bannister and Rudge, both with calf injuries, underwent fitness tests on the morning of the match, with Don Megson remarking that he could not afford to take the field with two players about whom there might be a fitness doubt, indicating that Dave Staniforth would return to the side. The £20,000 signing from Sheffield United had played five games and scored one goal since his transfer.

Aldershot were soon forced back on a bumpy pitch, with Rudge, under pressure, heading wide in the 4th minute. Then Kenny Stephens drove the ball past a crowd of players and goalkeeper Glen Johnson did well to save the winger's shot. Aldershot's first scoring attempt came from twenty-one-goal Jack Howarth after 24 minutes, when a delicately glanced header from full-back Richard Walden's centre was only inches off target. Rovers pressed again and eventually gained their reward in the 36th minute with a superbly taken Staniforth goal, starting the move himself with a pass to Trevor Jacobs on the touchline. John Rudge rose to the cross, Staniforth got in a second header from close range and then neatly brushed a shot into the net with the outside of his right foot from close in after Glen Johnson had palmed the ball out.

Rovers took only 3 minutes to add to their score in the second half, the goal coming from a free-kick by Trevor Jacobs. Staniforth, again in the action, headed towards the net and when goalkeeper Johnson again failed to grasp the ball, Richard Walden headed it off the line. The ball struck Staniforth on the chest and dropped for Rudge to tap the ball in from a yard out. Rudge's goal brought a brief show of Rovers' true worth and their revival contributed to a much-needed improvement in the standard of play, which was still below the level set by Rovers in the first half of the season.

Dave Staniforth fires the ball past Aldershot goalkeeper Glen Johnson to score Rovers' first goal.

John Rudge about to score his fifth goal of the season to clinch victory over Aldershot, watched by Rovers' other goalscorer Dave Staniforth.

Howarth should have narrowed the gap in the 70th minute with a header which he directed straight at Jim Eadie, the ball hitting the goalkeeper in the chest. With 7 minutes remaining Ron Walton stunned Rovers with a beautifully struck shot on the run which beat Eadie from a good 20yds, which brought unnecessary panic to Rovers for the final minutes. However, Aldershot were given few chances and it was Rovers who went close to scoring again when Rudge headed a Dobson corner on to the crossbar. It was a workmanlike, if unspectacular, display by the team that had led the Third Division for the past six months. The victory left them with a five-point lead at the top of the table with only six matches to go.

FRIDAY 5 APRIL 1974, HAIG AVENUE, SOUTHPORT

Southport	1 – Provan
Bristol Rovers	0
Half-time:	0-0
Attendance:	1,856
Referee:	Robin Clay (Gainsborough)
Southport:	Taylor, Sibbald, Ryder, Wright, Noble, O'Neil, Moore, Lloyd, Fryatt, Provan, Russell. Substitute: Hughes
Bristol Rovers:	Eadie, Jacobs, Parsons, Green, Taylor, Stanton, Stephens, O'Brien, Rudge, Staniforth, Dobson. Substitute: Bannister for Dobson (65 mins)

Needing six points from six games to clinch promotion, Don Megson switched the emphasis from power to skill for the Friday night match with relegation certainties Southport. Rovers' manager recalled touch-player Gerry O'Brien in place of the injured Frankie Prince and left Kenny Stephens and Colin Dobson on the two flanks, banking on creative ability to ensure victory. Southport, with only five League wins all season, were third from bottom of the division with twenty-six points.

Rovers could not get into their stride on a bone-hard pitch and striker Jim Fryatt, in his second spell with Southport, had some vigorous duels with Stuart Taylor. The in-form John Rudge put in the only goal-worthy shot in the opening 20 minutes, which carried an element of surprise about it, but goalkeeper Alan Taylor dealt with the situation and cut out the danger. Alex Russell set up the first scoring chance for Southport in the 27th minute with a pass out to Provan, who pulled the ball back perfectly to Norrie Lloyd, who hooked it over the bar from 6yds. In the 36th minute Tom Stanton came close to scoring for Rovers when he struck a first-time shot from a Kenny Stephens' centre which goalkeeper Taylor saved at the foot of the post. Five minutes later Colin Dobson found Rudge with a splendidly flighted corner and the striker headed goalwards from 16yds out, but Taylor again reacted smartly to tip the ball over the bar.

Soon after the start of the second half Lloyd was presented with a clear goalscoring chance when Mike Green headed the ball straight to his feet, but Lloyd volleyed yards wide with the whole goal to aim at. In the 54th minute Lloyd again found himself in the penalty area, but he miskicked when put through by Fryatt. Then a mistake by Dobson was intercepted by Provan, and when Fryatt shot, Jim Eadie appeared from nowhere to save. In the 61st minute Rovers paid the price for slack marking in defence when Fryatt moved in unmarked to reach a free-kick taken by Bobby Sibbald. He squeezed in a shot which rebounded off the far post, but inside-left Andy Provan ran in to score.

Dobson, after having a shot blocked by Taylor, was then taken off for Bannister and Rovers at long last found the form which had taken them to the top the table. Ten minutes from the end Alan Taylor made a point blank save from Bannister, turning the ball away for a corner, but it was Southport who carved out the openings with Lloyd missing yet another chance with a cross-drive when put clear with a beautifully placed lobbed pass by Provan.

Rovers not only received a severe blow to their pride, but had their Third Division championship hopes dented following this rock-bottom performance in which they were extremely fortunate not to have suffered their biggest defeat of the season. Ron Yeats, the former Liverpool centre half whose Tranmere side were Rovers' next opponents, left Haig Avenue well before the end of the game; he either believed that the leaders couldn't possibly play as badly again, or he felt he had seen enough to convince him that the team who had led the race all season had fallen apart.

FRIDAY 12 APRIL 1974, PRENTON PARK, BIRKENHEAD

Tranmere Rovers	0
Bristol Rovers	0
Half-time:	0-0
Attendance:	6,290
Referee:	Gordon Hill (Leicester)
Tranmere Rovers:	Johnson, Mathias, Farrimond, Moore, Yeats, Veitch, Peplow, Tynan, Mitchell, Crossley, Palios. Substitute: Allen
Bristol Rovers:	Eadie, Jacobs, Parsons, Green, Taylor, Prince, Stephens, Stanton, Warboys, Bannister, Dobson. Substitute: Rudge for Stephens (85 mins)

In the first of a three-match championship 'make-or-break' Easter programme, Rovers travelled to Birkenhead to face a Tranmere side still needing points to stay clear of relegation, and who were without leading scorer Tommy Young. Don Megson announced just before the team party left for the north that Alan Warboys was in the squad of thirteen players. Warboys had had two hard days in training earlier in the week and done well since, Megson remarking, 'I am pleased with his progress and with three matches to play, it has to be my decision which is the best time to bring him back'. The decision made, Warboys, who hadn't been in a losing Rovers side in a League match all season, was selected to lead the attack in his first full game for three months. Loan signing Gerry O'Brien was dropped again with Frankie Prince returning to midfield after injury.

After 10 minutes Tranmere player-manager and centre half Ron Yeats headed the ball into the Rovers' net, but referee Gordon Hill blew for an infringement and the goal was disallowed. Jim Eadie made a good save at the feet of Mark Palios after 25 minutes and soon afterwards Kenny Stephens' shot went wide of the goal after a pass by Bannister. Paul Crossley missed a good chance to put Tranmere ahead towards the end of the first-half when, with only Eadie to beat, he shot wide from 15yds when clear of an often-brittle Rovers defence.

Stuart Taylor leaps to head the ball clear against Tranmere Rovers during the 0-0 draw.

Alan Warboys lets fly with a left-foot shot during the Friday night game at Prenton Park.

More lucky escapes for Rovers came early in the second half; firstly Mitchell's close-range shot scorched over the bar after good approach work by Steve Peplow and Crossley; and then Peplow shot over the bar and then straight at Eadie when presented with two clear opportunities. Three minutes later Eadie made a good save from Mathias. Warboys came close to giving Rovers the lead when his fierce left-foot shot crashed against the bar with goalkeeper Johnson beaten, and with 5 minutes to go John Rudge came on for Stephens but there was nothing Rovers could do to find the net.

Rovers showed greater effort than they had at Southport, wingers Colin Dobson and Kenny Stephens being particularly industrious, but they rarely found any rhythm in midfield. The Pirates never dominated the game and it was indeed the lively Tranmere side who carved out the best chances; it did, however, give Rovers the psychological boost they so desperately needed. Manager Megson was satisfied with the result as another precious point towards promotion was safely in the bag, commenting, 'This result puts us in line for five points out of six over Easter. I was more worried about this game than I was about Oldham'.

SATURDAY 13 APRIL 1974, EASTVILLE STADIUM

Bristol Rovers	1 – Bannister
Oldham Athletic	2 – McVitie, Garwood
Half-time:	0-2
Attendance:	18,692
Referee:	John Yates (Redditch)
Bristol Rovers:	Eadie, Jacobs, Parsons, Green, Taylor, Prince, Stephens, Stanton, Warboys, Bannister, Dobson. Substitute: Rudge for Green (60 mins).
Oldham Athletic:	Ogden, Wood, Whittle, Blair, Hicks, Bailey, McVitie, Garwood, Lochhead, Robins, Groves. Substitute: Mulvaney for Blair (45 mins)

With ten away victories in eighteen games, Oldham could thank their performances at opponents' grounds for their handsome League position. The Latics, fresh from a 6-0 Friday night trouncing of relegation-threatened Southport, had two famous centre forwards on their playing staff. Andy Lochhead cost £20,000 when he was signed from Aston Villa, while Tony Hateley had been dogged by injury since he joined the club in July 1972. Rovers had the same twelve who were on duty in the draw at Tranmere for the vital Third Division championship clash, which meant the first home appearance by Alan Warboys since 22 February, when he scored the only goal of the victory over Watford.

Kenny Stephens unleashes a powerful shot at Eastville as Oldham full-back Ian Wood challenges.

Bruce Bannister heads Rovers' second-half goal from a corner in the table-topping clash with Oldham Athletic.

Rovers began with a flourish, forcing a corner in the opening moments as Whittle was forced to make a hurried clearance over his goal line. Rovers forced another corner as Warboys found Bannister with a header, but Dobson's kick was easily cleared. Then came a slick move started by Stanton with a good pass to Stephens on the right. He found Warboys, who fed the ball across the goalmouth to Dobson, who played the ball back to Stephens, whose crisp shot was saved by Ogden.

After 17 minutes Oldham took a shock lead with only their second attack of the game. Ian Woods' cross from the right was headed down by Lochhead to McVitie, who beat Eadie with a superbly struck shot from 2yds outside the penalty area. Rovers hit straight back with a tremendous drive from Stanton that Ogden pushed around for a corner, and Bannister got his head to a hooked volley by Warboys and headed just wide. Oldham were keeping things tight, and showing sharp striking power on their spasmodic sorties into Rovers' penalty area, and after 36 minutes dealt Rovers a shattering blow when they increased their lead. Andy Lochhead again played a major role feeding the ball to Robins, who touched it on to Blair. As Rovers' defence seemed slow to challenge, Colin Garwood had time to take possession and beat Eadie from close range.

After the interval, Rovers were not making enough impression on the visitors' defence to give any real hope of a comeback, and just on the hour Megson took off skipper Mike Green and brought on Rudge, with the intention of adding more striking power. Rudge's arrival triggered a period of intense Rovers' pressure, but Oldham's defence stayed cool and the game moved into its final quarter with Rovers still not having created a clear-cut chance. Garwood forged between Taylor and Parsons and forced Eadie to make a save with a low shot on the run. In the 77th minute, however, Rovers' hopes dramatically came back to life when Bannister brought them back in the game with a great header, turning Dobson's corner kick from the right just inside the far post, ensuring a tremendous finale to the championship clash.

Rovers fought all the way, and the support their fans gave them was tremendous, but on the day Oldham were the better side. Rovers' lead, once an impressive nine points, had now been whittled down to just one, and Oldham, with three games in hand, were poised to leapfrog the team they had been chasing all season.

TUESDAY 16 APRIL 1974, EASTVILLE STADIUM

Bristol Rovers	1 – Bannister
Tranmere Rovers	0
Half-time:	0-0
Attendance:	16,090
Referee:	Trevor Spencer (Wootton Bassett)
Bristol Rovers:	Eadie, Jacobs, Parsons, Aitken, Taylor, Prince, Stephens, Stanton, Warboys, Bannister, Rudge. Substitute: Staniforth for Stephens (80 mins)
Tranmere Rovers:	Johnson, Flood, Farrimond, Moore, Yeats, Veitch, Peplow, Tynan, Mitchell, Crossley, Young. Substitute: Palios for Crossley (70 mins)

The build-up to the final match of the Easter programme had Tranmere manager Ron Yeats predicting after Friday's goalless draw at Prenton Park that his in-form team would beat Rovers, with top scorer Tommy Young returning to the team having completed a two-match suspension. Don Megson brought in nineteen-year-old Peter Aitken in place of captain Mike Green, who had been substituted in the second half of the top-of-the-table clash with Oldham.

The uninspiring first-half consisted almost exclusively of a jittery Rovers side trying mainly to batter their way through a packed seven-man Tranmere defence. But Bruce Bannister's nineteenth goal of the season, 3 minutes into the second half, changed the whole complexion of the game. Alan Warboys, competitive as ever, swung a pass out to Kenny Stephens on the right. The winger raced down the touchline and flighted a perfect cross to the near post where Bannister's head met the ball and propelled it past Dick Johnson, despite the goalkeeper's valiant – and almost successful – attempt to save.

It was the first real goal effort from either side, and it set the scene for a more open and far more entertaining second half, restoring confidence to the Rovers team and bringing Tranmere out of their defensive shell. But Tranmere, superbly marshalled by their player-manager Ron Yeats, a former idol of Liverpool's Kop, had chances to save the game. After 50 minutes, a 15yd-volley from Eddie Flood, following a corner by Crossley, brought a brilliant save out of Jim Eadie when a goal looked certain, and 8 minutes later, Tynan laid on a gilt-edged chance only for Crossley to head wide from point-blank range.

The Tranmere fightback continued with a Yeats header just over the bar and a 'goal' by Tommy Young, which was disallowed for offside. Wrexham's defeat at Cambridge put them out of the promotion race as Rovers regained the leadership of the League, from which they had been deposed by Oldham the day before, and it was evident from the players' jubilation as the final whistle blew at Eastville that they felt the rich prize, which had slipped through Rovers' fingers so many times in recent years, was theirs at last. Despite the optimism of the delirious supporters massed around the dressing-room entrance, chanting Don Megson's name as the teams left the field, the manager was not ready to join the celebrations just yet: 'Chesterfield can still pip us if they win everything and we get nothing. We still need one point from our last two games to be sure,' said the Rovers boss.

BRISTOL ROVERS FOOTBALL CLUB LTD.

FOOTBALL LEAGUE—DIVISION 3

Bristol Rovers v. Tranmere Rovers

TUESDAY, 16th APRIL, 1974   Kick-off 7.30 p.m.

Block H   Row B Seat 2 2

NORTH STAND 80p   E. P. Terry

To be Retained

Secretary.

IN THE EVENT OF POSTPONEMENT THIS TICKET WILL BE AVAILABLE FOR THE RE-ARRANGED FIXTURE — NO MONEY WILL BE REFUNDED.
ANY ALTERATION IN KICK-OFF TIME WILL BE PUBLISHED IN THE LOCAL PRESS.

Match ticket for the Tranmere Rovers game.

Bruce Bannister heads in the match-winning goal past Tranmere's player-manager, Ron Yeats.

FRIDAY 19 APRIL 1974, ROOTS HALL, SOUTHEND

Southend United	0
Bristol Rovers	0
Half-time:	0-0
Attendance:	8,323
Referee:	Robert Perkin (Stafford)
Southend United:	Webster, Worthington, Ford, Elliott, Townsend, Moody, Coulson, Brace, Guthrie, Silvester, Johnson. Substitute: Dyer
Bristol Rovers:	Eadie, Jacobs, Parsons, Aitken, Taylor, Prince, Staniforth, Stanton, Warboys, Bannister, Rudge. Substitute: Fearnley

Needing just one more point to be certain of promotion to the Second Division, manager Don Megson linked up strikers Alan Warboys and Dave Staniforth, teammates at Sheffield United, for the first time in a Rovers side. With Bruce Bannister back in form during the previous two games, Rovers fielded three recognised strikers and supplemented the attacking strength from midfield by including John Rudge in a 4-3-3 formation. Peter Aitken was again preferred to Mike Green. Mid-table Southend, without a win in four at Roots Hall and losing the last two, kept the side that had secured victories at Walsall and Brighton.

The first half provided plenty of high-speed action with Southend doing most of the pressing, but there were precious few real chances at either end. After just 2 minutes Johnson hit a snap shot from the edge of the penalty area, but Eadie dealt with it capably. The Rovers defence was kept at full stretch as Southend powered forward, with Peter Aitken, star of Tuesday's win over Tranmere, again in fine form. It was from an Aitken lob that Rovers had their first tilt at goal after 13 minutes. Dave Staniforth, in for the injured Stephens, beat goalkeeper Malcolm Webster to the ball, but had it whipped off his foot by Moody before he had a chance to shoot. Aitken was again in action 3 minutes later to cut out a Silvester cross a spilt-second before it arrived at the feet of Southend's top scorer, Stuart Brace.

John Rudge slips a shot past defender Dave Worthington as Rovers attack the Southend goal.

Jubilant celebrations in the dressing room at Southend – with soft drinks only – after clinching promotion.

After 20 minutes, United's players had justifiable shouts for a penalty when Rovers' centre half Taylor appeared to handle the ball just inside the box, but the referee, Robert Perkin, turned down the appeals and waved play on. The closest Southend came to a first-half goal was after 21 minutes when a 25yd-'screamer' from Coulson flew inches over the Rovers' crossbar.

But as half-time approached, Southend's dominance started to fade and the early minutes of the second half belonged to Rovers.

However, again Southend started to press and Guthrie and Silvester both came close to scoring before Jim Eadie pulled off the save of the season. In the 74th minute, winger Billy Coulson sent Terry Johnson through, and his ferocious 22yd-shot looked a goal all the way, but somehow Eadie flung himself across his line to conjure the ball over the crossbar for a corner. The last thrill of a tremendously competitive second half came when Dave Staniforth, always dangerous, raced 50yds out of his own defence and cleverly beat Townsend, only to be foiled by goalkeeper Webster dashing out of the penalty area to kick to safety.

When the game ended and Rovers had won their precious point, hundreds of scarf-waving fans turned the pitch into a blue-and-white sea as they mobbed their heroes all the way to the dressing room. They had good cause to celebrate, for this dogged and hard-fought draw had regained Rovers the Second Division spot they had lost twelve years before. However, the success at Southend was marred a little when the players' coach broke down on the M4 near Chiswick on the journey home. A relief coach did not turn up, and it was not until nearly eight o'clock, having spent most of the night in a service station, that a third vehicle finally picked them up and dropped the tired but jubilant team at Eastville at ten o'clock on Saturday morning.

19 APRIL 1974

	P	W	D	L	F	A	Pts
ROVERS	45	22	16	7	64	32	60
York City	43	20	18	5	63	35	58
Oldham Athletic	41	24	10	7	75	42	58
Chesterfield	44	21	14	9	54	38	56
Wrexham	42	19	12	11	54	38	50
Bournemouth	43	16	14	13	52	54	46

SATURDAY 27 APRIL 1974, EASTVILLE STADIUM

Bristol Rovers   1 – Bannister (penalty)
Brighton & Hove Albion 1 – Robertson
Half-time: 0-1
Attendance: 19,137
Referee: Roy Capey (Madeley Heath)
Bristol Rovers: Eadie, Jacobs, Parsons, Green, Taylor, Prince, Rudge, Stanton, Warboys, Bannister, Dobson.
    Substitute: Staniforth for Dobson (75 mins)
Brighton & Hove Albion: Powney, Templeman, Wilson, Welch, Piper, Fuschillo, McEwan, Towner, Beamish, Robertson, O'Sullivan. Substitute: Howell (R)

Promotion gained, Rovers' players acknowledge the applause of the crowd prior to the final home game of the season.

In the lead-up to the final game, the eagerly-awaited return clash with Brian Clough's Brighton, there was great speculation amongst Rovers fans as to the line-up Don Megson would select for the grand finale of the season. Since the club clinched promotion with the goalless draw at Southend, excited Rovers fans had debated whether Megson would go back to the team that won nationwide fame with the televised thrashing of Brighton at the Goldstone Ground; or would he favour the line-up that played the most games in the record-equalling run of twenty-seven League games without defeat; or would he stick to the side that actually clinched the prize at Roots Hall? When the side was eventually announced to the thousands of fans who had come to pay tribute to the promotion heroes, captain Mike Green, who had lost his place for the last two games after leading the side all season, was reinstated. And it was Green who led the team out to receive a tremendous roar from the big crowd.

Rovers started nervously but went close following a foul on Dobson. Taylor moved up for the Parsons free-kick and headed just wide of the far post. Stanton then hit over a low cross from the right which Dobson cleverly back-heeled, but his attempt flashed inches wide of the far post. Brighton then began to emerge from

John Rudge leaps to meet a cross, with Brighton's defence massed to repel him.

their shell and a through-pass from Beamish ran well for McEwan, who shot powerfully on the run and Eadie needed two attempts to hold the ball. Then, after 19 minutes, Brighton snatched the lead when Towner's cross, from out on the right, was laid off by Robertson to Beamish. Robertson then darted in on a return pass to stroke the ball past Eadie from close range. Beamish went close to adding a second when he headed just wide from another Towner cross, and Rovers went close to equalising when Warboys did well to nod on a centre from Parsons to Rudge, who hit a first-time shot on to the outside of a post, and the ball bounced out for a goal kick.

Just before half-time, Brighton almost added to their lead when Fuschillo headed just wide. The sun had reappeared for the start of the second half, and Warboys blasted a 30yd-drive narrowly wide, before he then sent over a dangerous low cross which Templeman booted behind for a corner. Warboys then beat the offside trap to a Prince chip as Brighton's defence moved out, but Powney fisted the ball away from the striker's head. Brighton broke out to force a corner with an attack down the right and from O'Sullivan's inswinging kick, McEwan headed wide. Rovers continued to press forward, but made little impression on Brighton's defence until the 85th minute when Prince was brought down just inside the penalty area by Welch. From the resulting penalty, Bannister equalised as he sent Powney the wrong way.

Moments later Staniforth, on for Dobson, unleashed a flashing cross-shot but the ball went wide. As the final whistle blew, hundreds of fans swarmed onto the pitch as the players dashed to the dressing-room tunnel. But, within seconds, they reappeared in the Directors' Box to receive the adulation of their supporters and to strip off their shirts, as well as one pair of shorts, and throw them to the crowd.

There was then an extra roar as manager Don Megson appeared and thrust his arms high.

Bruce Bannister celebrates his point-saving penalty – his twentieth goal of the season – in the final League match against Brighton.

The Tote End in full voice celebrate Bannister's goal near the end of the game.

Rovers' players celebrate the end of the successful season by throwing their shirts into the crowd from the Directors' Box.

Jubilant fans celebrate in front of the South Stand.

29 APRIL 1974

	P	W	D	L	F	A	Pts
ROVERS	46	22	17	7	65	33	61
Oldham Athletic	44	25	11	8	83	45	61
York City	44	20	19	5	64	36	59
Chesterfield	46	21	14	11	55	42	56
Wrexham	45	21	12	12	61	42	54
Grimsby Town	46	18	15	13	67	50	51

With Rovers' League campaign completed and promotion gained, the Pirates could only wait for their two rivals to finish their fixtures to see what their final League position would be. Oldham had drawn 1-1 with York at Boundary Park on the Saturday, but there was a distinct possibility that Rovers would end the season in third place having led the division for most the season. But in two evening games on Tuesday 30 April, both York and Oldham were defeated: York lost 2-1 at Halifax, while Oldham were surprisingly beaten 2-0 at home by Charlton Athletic. The results guaranteed that Rovers would be at least runners-up as they had a goal average of 1.97, vastly superior to York City's 1.76.

The final twist in the remarkable season involved West Country rivals Plymouth Argyle playing both of the other promoted sides over a space of four days. Oldham travelled to Home Park on Friday 3 May needing one point to pip Rovers as champions of the Third Division, which they duly achieved following a goalless draw. A defeat by the Pilgrims would have put Rovers top of the table as Oldham's goal average of 1.77 was well short of Rovers' impressive figure. On Monday 6 May York beat Plymouth 2-0 to finish level on points with Rovers. Therefore, promotion was secured by champions Oldham Athletic, Bristol Rovers and York City, which at the time represented York's highest ever League finish. Rovers finished the season with the best defensive record in the division, conceding thirty-three goals, whilst Oldham scored an impressive eighty-three goals – fifty at home.

FINAL TABLE

	P	W	D	L	F	A	Pts
Oldham Athletic	46	25	12	9	83	47	62
ROVERS	46	22	17	7	65	33	61
York City	46	21	19	6	67	38	61
Wrexham	46	22	12	12	63	43	56
Chesterfield	46	21	14	11	55	42	56
Grimsby Town	46	18	15	13	67	50	51

GLOUCESTERSHIRE FA SENIOR PROFESSIONAL CUP FINAL
MONDAY 29 APRIL 1974, ASHTON GATE

Bristol City	0
Bristol Rovers	2 – Staniforth, Rudge
Half-time:	0-1
Attendance:	15,986
Referee:	Eric Read (Frampton Cotterell)
Bristol City:	Cashley, Sweeney, Drysdale, Gow, Collier, Merrick, Tainton, Mann, Cheesley, Gillies, Emmanuel. Substitutes: Whitehead for Gillies (52 mins) and Fear for Cheesley (59 mins)
Bristol Rovers:	Eadie, Jacobs, Parsons, Aitken, Taylor, Prince, Fearnley, Stanton, Warboys, Rudge, Staniforth. Substitute: Dobson for Fearnley (76 mins)

The end of season Gloucestershire FA Senior Professional Cup Final took on an extra significance for promotion heroes Rovers, as it was their first meeting with a Second Division club since they finally made certain of leaving the Third Division behind. The rivalry between Bristol's two League clubs is legendary and with City out to prove that they were still Bristol's premier club, and Rovers intent on showing they were more than ready for the challenge of Second Division football, there was added spice to the encounter. The previous two seasons needed penalty competitions to decide who took the cup. Rovers were without Bruce Bannister, who was unwell following an inoculation, while City dropped Keith Fear to make way for Jimmy Mann, signed from Leeds United on a free transfer. John Rudge gave an early warning to City when he robbed

Gordon Fearnley advances on the Bristol City goal during the 2-0 'Gloucester Cup' victory.

Dave Staniforth is tackled by City's Geoff Merrick in the 'Gloucester Cup' Final at Ashton Gate.

Gerry Gow and from a Gordon Fearnley centre Warboys out-jumped Brian Drysdale but headed over the bar.

The City midfield made another mistake in the 14th minute when Gerry Sweeney pushed the ball back weakly towards Gow and Frankie Prince intercepted. He sent Fearnley away down the left leaving Gary Collier stranded and as goalkeeper Cashley failed to hold his centre, Dave Staniforth turned smartly to score from close range. The goal came out of the blue, but it subsequently emphasised Rovers' superiority, pace, authority and composure, and although City fought furiously they were unable to outwit a well-disciplined defence. Paul Cheesley volleyed a Trevor Tainton centre high and wide, and Jim Eadie twice foiled City as he left his line to make stops early in the second half.

Alan Warboys set up the second Rovers goal with a short pass inside from the left, and Rudge eluded Emmanuel's lunge to aim a low, controlled drive for the near post from the inside-left position, 20yds out, and Rovers were coasting by the 53rd minute. After that it was just a question of playing out time before Stuart Taylor proudly received the trophy. The cup-tie atmosphere, with loud chanting from rival fans, and the thousands of gallons of water sprayed onto the pitch helped the game and the standard of play. Don Megson enthused that it was the best performance from his side for two months. John Rudge relished the laxity provided by City's early reliance on a 4-2-4 formation; Rovers had three men in midfield with Rudge as the spare man. With Alan Warboys, Dave Staniforth and Gordon Fearnley full of running and Frankie Prince prompting from behind, Rovers always looked the sharper, more positive side.

Jim Eadie's firm, solid punching, Stuart Taylor's total domination of the penalty area and Peter Aitken's accomplished reading of the game as sweeper negated all City's futile attacking sorties. So Rovers prepared for their summer tour confident in their ability to cope in the Second Division.

1973/74 LEAGUE APPEARANCES (SUBSTITUTE APPS IN BRACKETS)

Jim Eadie	46
Trevor Jacobs	46
Stuart Taylor	46
Tom Stanton	46
Bruce Bannister	44 (1)
Mike Green	44
Frankie Prince	43
Lindsay Parsons	42
Colin Dobson	39
Alan Warboys	32 (1)
Kenny Stephens	31
John Rudge	13 (6)
Gordon Fearnley	10 (6)
Dave Staniforth	8 (3)
Peter Aitken	6 (1)
Bryn Jones	4
Gerry O'Brien	3
Malcolm John	2 (1)
Jeff Coombes	1

LEAGUE GOALSCORERS

Alan Warboys	22
Bruce Bannister	18
John Rudge	4
Gordon Fearnley	3
Trevor Jacobs	3
Tom Stanton	3
Dave Staniforth	2
Stuart Taylor	2
Kenny Stephens	1
Colin Dobson	1
Mike Green	1
Malcolm John	1
Bryn Jones	1
Frankie Prince	1
Own goal (King)	1
Own goal (Wigginton)	1

SUBSTITUTES WITH APPEARANCES AND REPLACEMENTS

Gordon Fearnley	21	6	(Stephens five times, Eadie once)
John Rudge	9	6	(Staniforth twice, Dobson, Green, Parsons, Stephens once)
Malcolm John	6	1	(Dobson)
Dave Staniforth	3	3	(Bannister, Dobson, Stephens)
Peter Aitken	2	1	(Prince)
Bruce Bannister	1	1	(Dobson)
Bryn Jones	1	0	
Gerry O'Brien	1	0	
Kenny Stephens	1	0	
Alan Warboys	1	1	(O'Brien)

DIVISION THREE TOP GOALSCORERS 1973/74

Bill Jennings (Watford)	26
Jack Howarth (Aldershot)	25
Alan Gowling (Huddersfield)	24
Alan Warboys (Bristol Rovers)	22
Alan Buckley (Walsall)	21
Bruce Bannister (Bristol Rovers)	18
Stuart Brace (Southend United)	18
Arthur Horsfield (Charlton)	18
Chris Jones (York)	17
Ernie Moss (Chesterfield)	17
Jim Seal (York)	17

4

1973/74 AND ALL THAT

Radio Bristol sports reporter Colin Howlett, reviewing the season in the final match-day programme, considered that a football team's form away from home was essential to any success it hoped to achieve and was just as important as the strength of its reserves. The previous season promotion had been denied because of the lack of results on the grounds of opponents, just three away wins. Indeed, two of those were gained at the expense of teams later to be relegated – Swansea City and Scunthorpe United. For the first six months of the 1973/74 season things altered dramatically. The team set off at a tremendous pace at the start of the season and looked unbeatable as Rovers turned in performances in away matches that were overall more attractive to watch than the games at Eastville. The obvious reason for this was that the blanket defences they encountered at home stifled many of their most progressive ideas. Some of the exhibitions away from Bristol were outstanding, notably the wins at Bournemouth, Huddersfield and the never-to-be-forgotten December afternoon at Brighton. After the 2-1 win at Huddersfield, the home club's manager Ian Greaves was generous in defeat to the extent of remarking that on the evidence of that performance, Rovers were not only the best side in the Third Division, but better than most in the Second.

Throughout the autumn Don Megson's men were systematically securing the results essential to guarantee that this season, after all those frustrating near misses of previous campaigns, really was to be Rovers' promotion year. Jim Eadie improved on his previous season's feat of going five games without letting in a goal by conceding none in six matches and only one in nine games. Newcomer Trevor Jacobs immediately settled down as an ideal full-back partner for the ever-reliable Lindsay Parsons, while towering centre-halves Stuart Taylor and captain Mike Green commanded the penalty area. The tigerish tackling of Tom Stanton and Frankie Prince in midfield and the wing subtleties of Kenny Stephens and Colin Dobson ensured plenty of possession, on which the strong and powerful Alan Warboys and nippy and alert Bruce Bannister thrived, with Gordon Fearnley, Dave Staniforth and John Rudge more than adequate reinforcements, contributing much with some important goals.

However, Dame Fortune stopped coming to Bristol Rovers' away matches. Four in a row were lost, starting at Wrexham in February when what looked a perfectly good equalising goal by Bruce Bannister 5 minutes from time was disallowed. Then came Port Vale, and this time half the game was played without the services of injured goalkeeper Eadie, who had been carried off with concussion, necessitating skipper Mike Green making his first-ever appearance in goal. Two of the three goals conceded in the 3-1 defeat could be attributed to this, despite the valiant efforts of the captain. Two 1-0 defeats, at Plymouth Argyle with another disallowed goal in conditions upon which the Spanish Armada could have sailed, and up at York City, where Rovers lost by a controversial penalty in the fourth minute of injury time, upset morale.

It was only after the unbeaten run came to end after twenty-seven matches that Rovers began to falter. At the start of the season, a sort of 4-4-2 formation was adopted when defending, which significantly tightened up the 'goals against' number of the previous season. With both Warboys and Bannister scoring plenty of goals the team were able to defend very tightly, but when Warboys went out of the team with a hamstring injury the team lost quite a lot of its rhythm, missing the big striker's goalscoring and his strength in winning the ball. The team changed and the style of play adjusted, moving out of the groove which it had been in for so long. The problem now was that goals did not come so freely, and with more players going forward trying to score, this left the team more open at the back.

Like a front runner in the Grand National, Rovers began to peck at the final fences, and after topping the Third Division table for a record-breaking seven months they were overtaken in the ultimate sprint home. Rovers finally fell from their lofty perch after being beaten 1-0 by lowly Southport and 2-1 by Oldham in the Easter Saturday battle. At one stage, early in the New Year, Rovers had built an invincible-looking nine point lead at the top. Then things began to go a little awry, as Rovers stuttered slightly towards the end of the season. The loss of form coincided with the injury to Alan Warboys before the game at Wrexham, as his goalscoring skills had proved a major factor in the early-season successes. The troublesome hamstring from which he suffered caused him to miss twelve of the next thirteen matches, and although one player does not make a team, it is interesting to reflect upon the coincidence of his absence and Rovers' poor run. Remarkably, Warboys did not appear in a losing Rovers side in the League until the crunch encounter with Oldham Athletic.

Don Megson, commenting after the 2-0 reversal at home to Walsall which ended Rovers' unbeaten home run, remarked that the big cause for concern was the poor quality of the team's performance. There was no doubt in Megson's mind what the trouble was, 'There is so much apprehension about. It starts on the terraces and spreads on to the field. You could feel the tension in the stadium before a ball was kicked, and this seemed to communicate itself to our players on the pitch'.

Rovers' match-day programme for the vital Easter clash with Oldham Athletic.

However, the players were determined that nothing was going to ruin their promotion bid this season, and two of the greatest factors in this dream being realised were the calm leadership of Don Megson and the pleasant Scots humour of trainer-coach Bobby Campbell. When Megson was appointed Rovers' manager in 1972 he said, 'I want us to become the Leeds United of the Third Division', and it was an interesting quirk of fate that the records of the two sides should have been so similar. For a long time they were the only unbeaten sides in the League – and both saw handsome leads in their respective divisions eroded away at the tail-end of the season. As a result of Leeds' superb form and record First Division unbeaten run, Rovers equally impressive and scintillating displays did not receive the full accolades and attention they so obviously deserved. One of the most decisive improvements made by Megson was to tighten Rovers' defence, and as a consequence only thirty-three goals were conceded in the forty-six League games – fewer than any other team in the Third Division. It was also the lowest in the club's history, breaking the previous best of thirty-six in forty-two games back in the 1922/23 season.

The disappointing late-season results cast a slight shadow over Rovers' earlier brilliance, but despite finishing in a less confident manner, Rovers' rivals for promotion were still five points behind at the end of the season. The injury to Warboys, which caused him to miss fifteen matches, may have been a factor, but probably the truth was that such a hot pace had been set in the autumn that it was virtually beyond the realms of human capability for it to be maintained throughout a strenuous nine-month British season. When one looks back on the season, it is too easy to remember the frustrating, nail-biting, cliff-hanging finish and forget the splendid run which preceded it.

Much of the credit for the club's success must undoubtedly be given to Don Megson who, as well as demonstrating a shrewd tactical brain, had inspired and motivated his players to great heights. In addition, Megson gave the players a sense of importance, and one of his first actions on becoming manager was to institute the practice of gathering the team together at a motel on the outskirts of Bristol prior to every home fixture for a pre-match lunch. Besides helping to generate a greater feeling of team spirit and allowing the manager more time to mould everyone's

Don Megson receives his September Bell's Whisky 'Third Division Manager of the Month' award.

approach to the game, it also brought a touch of First Division style to Bristol Rovers. Before the early kick-offs due to the national fuel emergency, a proportion of away games were journeyed to on the Saturday morning, with lunch at about 12.30 p.m. at a hotel reasonably close to the ground, leaving the players plenty of time to dine and relax before the serious business of the afternoon. Port Vale was just about as far north as the team would travel on the same day as the match, Megson believing that longer trips would not leave the players enough time to unwind unless an overnight stay was made.

Unlike his predecessor, Megson installed a sense of solid defending with quick counter-attacking; he preferred a 1-0 win to a high scoring encounter, deciding to use strength and determination rather than sheer flair and football ability to get out of the Third Division. He had his critics, but he succeeded in managing a successful return to Division Two in 1974 and later establishing Rovers in the higher division. However, all this would not have been possible but for the fact that Megson inherited a club that had been put on a firm financial footing and already possessed a talented pool of players. These crucial foundation stones had been laid many years earlier by, amongst others, such men as Bert Tann, Fred Ford, Bill Dodgin and Bobby Campbell.

Rovers' second promotion triumph in 1974 was greeted with acclaim by all football followers as they had followed and stuck to a style of play which was exemplified by hard work. The terrace supporter was fond of the employment of wingers Colin Dobson and Kenny Stephens, who created countless goalscoring opportunities. Promotion had been achieved through a consistent spell of good results with the team practically selecting itself. Whether winning or losing, Don Megson's men commanded tremendous respect during the campaign, and whilst to the nationwide public they made their mark with the televised 8-2 trouncing of Brighton, within the game itself those goalless draws and 1-0 victories impressed rival managers and players just as much. No team had made such an impact on the Third Division for a very long time and Rovers were considered to be the 'Leeds United of the Third Division'. And that's why, when the run of unbeaten League games was finally ended at the Racecourse Ground one match short of creating a new record for the grade, a disgruntled Mike Green commented: 'You'd have thought they had just won the Cup final'. That first defeat in twenty-eight League matches was hard to take, particularly in the circumstances in which it came. Five minutes from the end, Bruce Bannister equalised, but the goal was disallowed – a decision Rovers' lads are still ready to dispute today.

Despite the good start to the 1973/74 season, there had been a great deal of talk in the local press of transfers involving Bristol Rovers. As early as September Megson denied that he had received any bids for Bruce Bannister, several First Division clubs having watched the twenty-five-year old striker, who made no secret of his desire to play First Division football. However, the Rovers manager was searching for an experienced midfield player to strengthen his squad and having failed to attract former England international Peter Thompson from Liverpool, he looked at Alan Durban of Derby County, but considered that the former Welsh international was not the type needed in the side. There were also hopes that Megson could attract Tottenham's midfielder Phil Holder to Rovers. In February, Ernie Machin, the Plymouth captain who had led his side to the League Cup semi-finals, was being talked of as a potential midfield signing by Megson. The skilful twenty-nine-year-old schemer, who cost Argyle £40,000, was keen to move nearer to Coventry, where he had strong ties.

In the end, however, at the beginning of March Megson recruited another striker, signing Sheffield United's Dave Staniforth, the £20,000 forward considered by the Rovers' boss as a promotion insurance policy, underling the manager's concern about the seriousness of Warboys' injury. Staniforth signed for Rovers with 20 minutes to spare before the 9.10 p.m. transfer deadline – giving Megson the required forty-eight hours to register the player with the Football League. Rovers' manager clinched the deal after dashing to the Europa Hotel in West Bromwich to meet Staniforth halfway. A few weeks later Gerry O'Brien, the twenty-three-year-old Southampton winger or midfield player, joined Rovers on loan, with Megson, Southampton boss Lawrie McMenemy and the player reaching agreement at The Dell just before the transfer deadline. Valued at £40,000, Megson revealed that he viewed the acquisition as much as a signing for the future as an injection of extra talent to the squad: 'I believe in temporary transfers only when there is a real possibility of them becoming permanent. This is what I have in mind for Gerry,' commented the Rovers boss, but ultimately the Scot returned to Southampton a little disillusioned with his spell at Eastville.

Indeed, Megson himself was the subject of much press speculation regarding a move away from Eastville. As early as November, Megson, halfway through his three-year contract, was being linked with both Sheffield clubs; at United to replace John Harris and by his former club Wednesday after they slid to the lower regions of the Second Division. Megson was also being linked with the managerial vacancy at First Division Norwich City, but following the sacking of Hillsborough boss Derek Dooley on Christmas Eve there was great speculation as to whether he would apply for the Wednesday job with eighteen months of his contract still to run. In the end Steve Burtenshaw was appointed manager at Hillsborough with John Bond taking over at Carrow Road, while Ken Furphy becoming boss of Sheffield United.

Throughout the season there were numerous references in the newspapers, match-day programmes and by Megson himself to the tremendous support Rovers received, particularly at away games where home attendances increased considerably wherever Rovers played. The team could always rely upon tremendous vocal support during their home games at Eastville, particularly the singing and noise generated by the famous Tote End. The average attendance at Eastville was 13,508 spectators, with an average away crowd of 8,424, with just under half a million fans watching Rovers' forty-six League games. However, this was a period when football hooliganism was perceived as being at its peak and Peter Terry, reflecting on his first year as Bristol Rovers Secretary, made reference to the small number of so-called followers who 'are more trouble than they are worth', wondering if these youngsters realised the cost they force their clubs to undertake in extra police and security arrangements to enable the majority to enjoy their football. Megson, commenting in the Watford programme, mentioned the crowd trouble that occurred at Port Vale, and there were crowd problems at Aldershot and on the Rovers' Supporters' Club chartered train on the return from York City. At Northampton, in the FA Cup, the referee threatened to abandon the match when fans caused trouble on the pitch.

But unruly spectators at football matches wasn't the only difficulty football clubs had to deal with during the 19734/74 season. A political crisis, which affected the League programme, stemmed from the support of Western countries for Israel in the Arab-Israeli War of October 1973. In response, the Arab countries introduced a boycott of fuel supplies, subsequently replacing this with substantial price increases through OPEC. Western countries were thrown into crisis and although the United Kingdom was not perhaps as dependent on oil as some, the National Union of Mine Workers introduced an overtime ban on 12 November 1973 in pursuit of a pay claim, as did key workers in the electricity industry. The response of the government was to declare a state of emergency and from 14 November a series of measures were introduced to restrict fuel consumption, one of which related to the use of floodlights for sporting events. Thus, from Saturday 14 November, all Football League fixtures kicked off at 2.15 p.m. rather than 3 p.m., and then with the darker nights drawing in this soon went back to 2 p.m. Clubs could hire (or buy) generators to power the floodlights and some did so, thus enabling them to kick-off at 3 p.m.

A month after the introduction of the restrictions the political crisis stepped up a level and on 13 December the government announced even more stringent measures. In the period between Monday 17 and Sunday 31 December, industrial and commercial concerns were to be allowed five days of normal fuel consumption, and then from 1 January they were limited to a maximum of three specific consecutive days of fuel, and thus the three-day working week was introduced. The Football League Management Committee considered, and quickly rejected, the possibility of a winter break. Although clubs were able to use their floodlights over the holiday period, they could no longer use private generators to power the lights for matches.

Rovers' first home fixture to be affected by the floodlight ban was the Southend United game which kicked off at 2 p.m., the revised start time continuing until 23 February when the game against Watford reverted to the traditional 3 p.m. kick-off. The welcome return of floodlit football to Eastville, on 5 March against Rochdale after a four-month break, was due entirely to the determination of secretary Peter Terry and commercial manager Keith Hunt. Their efforts to acquire a generator against seemingly insuperable odds finally succeeded and Don Megson was able to complete his fixture arrangements satisfactorily without sacrificing the first stage of the club's worldwide tour in May, remarking that the acquisition of a generator for midweek games 'means that more of our fans will be able to watch the matches and that I can space out the fixtures to avoid a late congestion of games'.

Interestingly, Rovers' forty-six League fixtures took place on six of the seven days of the week, Thursday being the only day that Rovers didn't play a game during 1973/74. Two away games (vs Aldershot and Port Vale) were played on a Sunday; the match at Rochdale on a Monday evening; ten fixtures were completed on Rovers' normal Tuesday evening slot; Hereford away and Plymouth home on Boxing Day took place on a Wednesday; and Friday saw three away trips to Southport, Tranmere, and Southend, together with the home match against Huddersfield. The traditional Saturday fixture accounted for the remaining twenty-seven matches.

Keith Hunt, Rovers' new commercial manager, was instrumental in a number of novel commercial activities aimed at obtaining badly needed funds for the club, as well as raising its profile. Rovers, with an eye to increasing their revenue and projecting the modern go-ahead image of a progressive football club, appointed Hunt in July 1973, and it was Hunt who promoted Warboys and Bannister, producing 'Smash and Grab' pictures, posters and scarves which were sold in the Development Association shop.

Rovers' commercial department produced 'Beware of Smash & Grab' posters.

Left: Rod Hull and 'Emu' show their support for Bristol Rovers.

Below: Rovers' players enjoy a Christmas party at Eastville with their families.

Another venture was the release of a single 'Bristol Rovers All The Way' recorded with Rod Hull and his manic bird 'Emu', who were appearing in the pantomime *Aladdin* at the Bristol Hippodrome. The idea came after the pair, along with entertainer Larry Grayson, were invited to the players' Christmas party in the Beaufort Room at Eastville on 2 January. The 'cutting' of the single necessitated that the players, Eastville staff and Hull travelled to EMI's London recording studio.

The record was first released in New Zealand and Australia to coincide with the club's tour and then in the UK. However, needless to say, the song, to the tune of 'She'll Be Coming Round the Mountain' didn't make the pop charts. In March, Rovers jointly promoted a Glenn Campbell concert at the Bristol Hippodrome, the event attracting two capacity houses of over 4,000 people. The American singer adapted the words of his latest record 'London' to 'Bristol' and dedicated it to Rovers in their promotion run. This was followed in June by Rovers presenting a Barclay James Harvest concert. Car sponsorship deals were also arranged for Bannister, Warboys and Tommy Stanton.

Right: Don Megson with his wife, Yvonne, and son, Neil, who went on to represent USA at football and manage several clubs there.

Below: Kenny Stephens, Dave Staniforth, Lindsay Parsons, Trevor Jacobs and Dick Sheppard, in London to record 'Bristol Rovers All The Way', pose in Carnaby Street.

Before the days of replica kits and numerous changes of strips by football teams, and when goalkeepers wore green jerseys, Rovers uncharacteristically for that period wore five different kits during 1973/74: the new blue-and-white-quartered shirts with white shorts; white shirts with black shorts; red-and-white shirts with black shorts; blue shirts with white shorts (at Tranmere); and the gold shirts and black shorts worn on just one occasion at Brighton, allegedly burnt by Brian Clough following his side's heavy defeat.

For a Third Division club, Rovers had more than their fair share of national exposure through televised coverage of their games. Highlights of all of the pre-season Watney Cup games were broadcast by the BBC, as was the case each season the competition ran. The table-topping clash with local West Country rivals Bournemouth was featured on Saturday night's *Match of the Day* and the most talked about victory of the season, the 8-2 beating of Brian Clough's side at Brighton, was the main match on the *Big Match* broadcast on the Sunday afternoon.

'Smash and Grab'

The combination of Alan Warboys and Bruce Bannister brought Rovers more than forty of their goals, handsomely repaying the £58,000 which the club spent on bringing them to Eastville, where Rovers' twin strikers became the most feared forwards in the Third Division that season. December brought them their biggest haul, with a total of sixteen goals, but the match at Brighton on the first day of December will always be remembered as their most memorable raid, where, to the delight of millions of television viewers, Warboys smashed four and Bannister grabbed three. By early February they had collected no less than thirty-five goals between them. In one electrifying spell of four League games Warboys hit ten goals – hat-tricks against Southport and Southend, and the four against Brighton. The break-up of the striking duo, which came when Warboys suffered his hamstring injury in early February, put a fierce brake on Rovers' stampede at the top of the table.

It was Rovers' newly appointed commercial manager Keith Hunt, searching for a slogan, who dreamed up the title 'Smash and Grab' for Rovers' potent strikeforce. Besides posters and scarves, a more tangible reward for their fame brought about by the televised Brighton game was the presentation of two cars to Bannister and Warboys by Welch & Co. The keys to the two new vehicles were presented to the duo prior to the start of the Watford match in October – Warboys receiving a Vauxhall Magnum and Bannister an Opel Manta.

Bannister received an Opel Manta and Warboys a Vauxhall Magnum in a sponsorship deal with Welch & Co.

In March, Warboys and Bannister were chosen by their fellow professionals as the best strikers in the Third Division, the players receiving specially inscribed silver medals, with former Rovers skipper Brian Godfrey, now with Newport County, voted into the Fourth Division's outstanding team.

In interviews given in March 2006 to Lee Honeyball, of the *Observer Sport Monthly*, 'Smash and Grab' recalled their time at Eastville:

Warboys:

I loved my time at Bristol Rovers because it was such a family club. There used to be a dog track around the pitch at Eastville with a bar area where all the players would go with their families every Friday afternoon. All the kids sat at one table while the players and their wives were at another. Bruce was already at the club when I arrived, in March 1973, and that's when our friendship started.

Bannister:

Within a few games we had struck up an understanding and once things started happening for us on the pitch it snowballed. In the November the club came up with the 'Smash and Grab' idea and made Wild West-style posters of us. I've still got one. Our next game after the posters came out was away at Brighton, where Brian Clough had just taken over. We were in the middle of going twenty-seven games unbeaten from the start of the season and when Chelsea's game against Leeds, who also hadn't lost all season, was cancelled, all the attention turned to our match. The ground was packed because there were no games in London and twenty were called off overall through bad weather. I ended up getting a first-half hat-trick and Alan scored four. The 8-2 win made our name.

Warboys:

It was an unbelievable performance. I finished with a cut eye and needed stitches. While I was on the treatment table Cloughie walked in. He told me that the cut must have been self-inflicted, because his defenders hadn't been near me all afternoon.

Bannister:

They even made 'Smash and Grab' scarves after that game.

Warboys:

I was the old-fashioned target man who used to fight for every ball, while Bruce picked up the pieces. As long as I made a nuisance of myself, I didn't even have to win the ball because Bruce would always be on to it. We had a winger called Kenny Stephens who used to whip crosses in. I went to the back post while Bruce attacked the near post.

Bannister:

Kenny would sell that many dummies that he could be a real pain. Great player, though.

Warboys:

Our partnership was so successful that it was obvious when, in 1976/77, it started to dip. That's when they off-loaded us. I'd started to slow down a bit. Fulham had George Best, Bobby Moore, Rodney Marsh and Peter Storey, so I jumped at the chance to join them. All they wanted was a big fella up front to take the knocks. Bestie used to train in the afternoons instead of mornings so I'd stay behind just to watch. You've never seen a rush like when we played five-a-sides: everyone wanted to be on his team. I moved to Hull the next season and guess who was already there...

Bannister:

I'd moved there after a short spell with Plymouth. Our partnership wasn't quite as good at Hull – we were older. But it was nice to be alongside Alan again. I finished my career at Dunkirk and, from there, worked for the Professional Footballers' Association. I started my sports shoe store around the time of the jogging boom in the early Eighties and it grew from there. We now do most of our business online.

Warboys:

When I finished playing, I was badly let down by Doncaster Rovers. I had started my career there and wanted to stay in football. They said there would always be a job for me but, when the time came, there was nothing. I was so disillusioned that I left football and, after a year out, I ran a pub. Then I became a lorry driver. It suits me: I never do long distances and I'm home every night.

Bannister:

We've been friends for more than thirty years and we've stayed in touch. Our wives are friends and we meet up whenever we can. But we rarely talk about old times: we were both there and know what happened.

Alan 'Smash' Warboys and Bruce 'Grab' Bannister reunited in 2010.

Summer Tour

On the morning of 4 May a party of sixteen players and five officials left Eastville Stadium by coach on the first part of a four-week, seven-match tour to Australia, New Zealand and Thailand. It was the first major tour to be undertaken by Bristol Rovers. After watching the FA Cup Final on television at London Airport the squad flew to Frankfurt for an overnight stay before catching a Sydney-bound DC10. Four games were played during a fifteen-day stay in Australia – at Brisbane, Sydney, Newcastle and Melbourne. The playing record was: won 3, lost 1, goals for 15, goals against 4, the only defeat coming through a goal from the last kick of the game in Victoria. One disappointment for the tour party was that Rovers never played the Australian national side, as was originally arranged, because as they had qualified for the World Cup they did not want to take undue risk of injury. However, the team they met in Sydney contained nine of their World Cup pool players.

THURSDAY 9 MAY 1974, EXHIBITION GROUND, BRISBANE

Queensland	1 – Spiekerman (68 mins)
Bristol Rovers	2 – Bannister (81 mins), Staniforth (90 mins)
Half-time:	0-0
Queensland:	Jones, Wilkins, Knott, Edwards, Sunderland, Schneider, Fagan, Marley, Dench, Spiekerman, McCabe. Substitutes: Kelly for Jones, Steel, Strawson
Bristol Rovers:	included Jim Eadie, Stuart Taylor, Peter Aitken, Dave Staniforth and Bruce Bannister (no full record of the line-up)

The opening game was played against the Queensland representative side on Thursday 9 May 1974 at the Exhibition Ground, Brisbane, the Eastville side clinching victory with a hotly disputed goal, claimed to be offside, in the last minute of the match.

When the Eastville side arrived in Sydney for their midweek game with New South Wales, they found the New Zealand rugby team, the famous All Blacks, booked in at the same hotel. Rovers' players shared training facilities with the New Zealanders and a match was arranged between the two groups; one half was played under association football rules, the other half using the rugby football code.

Rovers' squad photographed with the New Zealand All Blacks rugby team poolside at the Sydney hotel they shared.

WEDNESDAY 15 MAY 1974, SYDNEY SPORTS GROUND, NEW SOUTH WALES

New South Wales	0
Bristol Rovers	3 – Bannister (4 mins), Stephens (53 mins), Watkins – own goal (78 mins)
Half-time:	1-0
Attendance:	4,481
Referee:	Tim Davies (New South Wales)
New South Wales:	Allan Maher (Jimmy Fraser 46 mins), Robert McGinn, Ivo Rudic, John Watkiss, Harry Williams, Alan Ainslie, Ernie Campbell, David Harding, Billy Rogers, Adrian Alston, Terry Butler. Substitute: Col Bennett for Rogers (60 mins). Coach: Leo Baumgartner
Bristol Rovers:	Eadie, Jacobs, Parsons, Aitken, Taylor, Prince, Stephens, Stanton, Warboys, Bannister, Dobson. Substitutes: Staniforth for Stephens (60 mins), Fearnley for Warboys (79 mins). Rudge for Dobson (70 mins)

The match against the New South Wales state representative side was staged on the eve of the Socceroos' World Cup departure for the finals in Germany, and included nine members of Australia's World Cup squad.

THURSDAY 16 MAY 1974, WESTON PARK, WESTON, NEW SOUTH WALES

Coalfields XI	1 – (scorer not known)
Bristol Rovers	9 – Warboys (2), Staniforth (2), Bannister (2), Rudge (2), Sneddon (own goal)
Attendance:	6,000
Coalfields XI:	John Hogg, Graham King, Paul Robertson, Ken Boardman, Tom Arrowsmith, Peter Irving, John Bond, Roy Johnson, Tom Sneddon, Warren Halverson, Kerr McLerries. Substitutes: Jim Goldsmith for Hogg (46 mins), Graham Payne, Terry Dobson
Bristol Rovers:	included John Rudge, Stuart Taylor, Peter Aitken, Frank Prince, Alan Warboys, Dave Staniforth and Bruce Bannister

The Coalfields XI team was composed predominantly of players from the Weston club in Newcastle, New South Wales, with some guest players from Cessnock and Maitland.

SUNDAY 19 MAY 1974, OLYMPIC PARK, MELBOURNE, VICTORIA

Victoria	2 – Howie (55 mins), Armstrong (90 mins)
Bristol Rovers	1 – Fearnley (44 mins)
Half-time:	1-0
Attendance:	6,000
Victoria:	Lou Kastner, Mike Pye, Steve Walker, Andrew Kazi, Jim Tansey, John Howie, Frank Micic, Pat Bannon, Steve Bleskany, Mike Micevski, Joe Palinkas. Substitutes: George Gillan for Bleskany (46 mins), Jim Armstrong for Micevski (62 mins). Coach: Tony Boggi
Bristol Rovers:	Eadie, Jacobs, Parsons, Aitken, Taylor, Prince, Rudge, Stanton, Staniforth, Bannister, Fearnley. Substitutes: Sheppard for Eadie (46 mins), Stephens for Stanton (62 mins), Dobson for Fearnley (62 mins)

The final match against representative teams on the East Coast was against the Victorian state side at Olympic Park.

In New Zealand Rovers played three games against provincial sides, being victorious in all three, scoring nine goals and conceding none.

WEDNESDAY 22 MAY 1974, ENGLISH PARK, CHRISTCHURCH

Canterbury	0
Bristol Rovers	3 – Rudge, Bannister, Warboys
Half-time:	0-1

The first goal came in the first minute of play when a Canterbury defender missed a header after John Rudge floated the ball in from 35yds out. Rovers' other goals came within a minute of each other in the second half, Bannister scored the first and Warboys the second. Canterbury missed a second-half penalty.

Programme cover for Rovers' tour match against
Canterbury in New Zealand.

SOCCER
SPECIAL

OFFICIAL PROGRAMME   PRICE 20c

ENGLISH PARK 22nd MAY, 1974

THE N.Z. FOOTBALL ASSOCIATION

PRESENTS

INTERNATIONAL SOCCER

BRISTOL ROVERS
v.
CANTERBURY

KICK-OFF—7.30 p.m.

SATURDAY 25 MAY 1974, WELLINGTON

Wellington	0
Bristol Rovers	4 – Bannister (2), Fearnley, Stephens
Half-time:	0-3

Rovers scored through Fearnley and Bannister twice in the first half, and Kenny Stephens netted the fourth with a 30yd-shot a minute from the final whistle.

SUNDAY 26 MAY 1974, NEWMARKET PARK, AUCKLAND

Auckland	0
Bristol Rovers	2

According to Bobby Campbell, the hardest match of the whole tour was at Auckland, which was won 2-0, against a team managed by an old pal from his Chelsea days, Ken Armstrong.

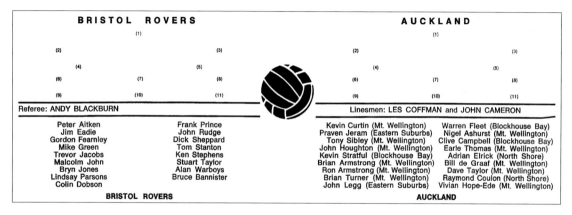

The Bristol Rovers and Auckland squads as they appeared in the match-day programme.

BRISTOL ROVERS' SUPPORTERS' CLUB

0 00

The Chairman and Committee
request the pleasure of the company of

....

at the

PROMOTION DINNER AND DANCE

to be held at

The Mayfair Banqueting Suite, Frogmore Street, Bristol 1.

on WEDNESDAY, 5th JUNE, 1974

R.S.V.P

57, Mangotsfield Road,
Staple Hill, Bristol, BS16 5NA

7.30 p.m. for 8.00 p.m.
Dress Optional

FOOTBALL LEAGUE FINAL TABLE

DIVISION III

									PLAYERS WHO APPEARED IN THE PROMOTION TEAM
Oldham ...	...	...	46	25	12	9	83	47	62	PETER AITKEN
BRISTOL ROVERS ...	...	46	22	17	7	65	33	61	BRUCE BANNISTER
York ...	...	...	46	21	19	6	67	38	61	JEFF COOMBES
Wrexham	...	...	46	22	12	12	63	43	56	COLIN DOBSON
Chesterfield	...	...	46	21	14	11	55	42	56	JIM EADIE
Grimsby	...	...	46	18	15	13	67	50	51	GORDON FEARNLEY
Watford	...	...	46	19	12	15	64	56	50	MIKE GREEN
Aldershot	...	...	46	19	11	16	65	52	49	TREVOR JACOBS
Halifax ...	...	...	46	14	21	11	48	51	49	MALCOLM JOHN
Huddersfield	...	...	46	17	13	16	56	55	47	LINDSAY PARSONS
Bournemouth	...	...	46	16	15	15	54	58	47	FRANKIE PRINCE
Southend	...	...	46	16	14	16	62	62	46	JOHN RUDGE
Blackburn	...	...	46	18	10	18	62	64	46	TOM STANTON
Charlton	...	...	46	19	8	19	66	73	46	KENNY STEPHENS
Walsall ...	...	...	46	16	13	17	57	48	45	STUART TAYLOR
Tranmere	...	...	46	15	15	16	50	44	45	ALAN WARBOYS
Plymouth	...	...	46	17	10	19	59	54	44	BRYN JONES
Hereford	...	...	46	14	15	17	53	57	43	DAVID STANIFORTH
Brighton...	...	...	46	16	11	19	52	58	43	GERRY O'BRIEN
Port Vale	...	...	46	14	14	18	52	58	42	
Cambridge	...	...	46	13	9	24	48	81	35	
Shrewsbury	...	...	46	10	11	25	41	62	31	
Southport	...	...	46	6	16	24	35	82	28	
Rochdale	...	...	46	2	17	27	38	94	21	

AUTOGRAPHS

Left: Invitation to Rovers' Supporters' Club promotion celebration dinner and dance at the Mayfair Suite.

Below: Rovers' Chairman Douglas Mearns Milne enjoys a drink with Bannister, Warboys and Eadie at the York National Railway Museum.

The Auckland representative side was made up of players from National League teams Blockhouse Bay, Eastern Suburbs, Mt Wellington and North Shore United. Rovers' manager, Don Megson, was last seen at Newmarket Park in June 1969 when he captained a touring English FA XI which beat New Zealand 5-0.

The final port of call was Thailand, where just the one game was played in terrific heat and at a slower pace than usual.

THURSDAY 30 MAY 1974, NATIONAL STADIUM, BANGKOK

Bangkok XI	2 – Srisavat, (other scorer not known)
Bristol Rovers	4 – Bannister (3), Warboys
Half-time:	1-0
Attendance:	3,000

Rovers trailed 1-0 at half-time, but Alan Warboys equalised with a header just after the restart before the home team went ahead again with a shot from right-winger Nivat Srisavat. Rovers then took command and Bannister scored a hat-trick, bringing his total on the tour to ten goals.

Despite Rovers making a loss of £5,000 on the trip, manager Don Megson felt the tour had been worthwhile and the money well spent, as it had produced a number of dividends: useful information was gleaned from playing some games with a 4-2-4 formation, others with 4-3-3 and watching how players adapted; Bruce Bannister got back among the goals, scoring in every game but one and snapping up chances smartly after failing to reach the target he set himself during the promotion season; John Rudge continued the tremendous form he showed as a midfield player just before the tour started; Colin Dobson's foot stood up well to the hard grounds, suggesting his long-standing injury problem was over; Dick Sheppard's outstanding game against Auckland, including two brave saves at the feet of forwards, proved he was ready to make his first-team comeback for Rovers.

Coming home from the successful antipodean tour, the promotion team were honoured by Bristol Rovers Supporters' Club at a Promotion Dinner held at the Mayfair Banqueting Suite on 5 June. After the meal, which included 'Promotion Sherry Trifle' and 'Apple Pie a La Mode Second Division', the players and senior staff members were presented with inscribed silver tankards, and Chairman Douglas Mearns Milne was given a commemorative silver rose bowl. At the end of speeches, manager Don Megson led the players in a round of applause in appreciation of the wonderful backing they had been given by the fans, especially away from home.

There was also a celebration dinner held at the Grand Hotel in Bristol, the ballroom bedecked with blue-and-white, with the waitresses wearing the famous quartered shirts, attended by 350 guests including the Lord Mayor, Bert Peglar. Other guests included the heads of all departments at Eastville – turnstile men, programme sellers, commissionaires – and as well as the full compliment of Bristol City directors, representatives of Bristol Rugby Club and Gloucestershire Cricket Club were also present. Alan Warboys was presented with the Player of the Year Trophy.

5

TOUGH IN DIVISION TWO

Peter Aitken played in all the games during the summer trip to Australia and New Zealand and Megson must have gained a favourable impression of the young defender because just before the start of the 1974/75 season he sold Mike Green to Plymouth Argyle for a £19,000 fee, where at the end of the season the former captain again tasted Third Division promotion success with the Devon side. With the departure of Green, Stuart Taylor was appointed club captain in preference to Frankie Prince and John Rudge. However, the player who had led Rovers into the Second Division was soon back at Eastville as the Pilgrims were Rovers' opponents in the first round of the League Cup on 20 August. The match ended in a 0-0 draw, with the replay at Home Park settled by an Alan Warboys goal 4 minutes from time. Luton then defeated Rovers at Kenilworth Road in the next round.

A largely familiar-looking Rovers side took a point off Notts County before an opening-day Eastville crowd of 14,365 and there was a brief honeymoon period, Rovers remaining unbeaten for three games. The first away fixture of the Second Division campaign saw Rovers travel to Hillsborough on Saturday 24 August 1974 to take on Sheffield Wednesday, the club which manager Don Megson had served with such distinction, being heralded as one of the greatest servants of the Owls. Megson, by his own admission, didn't normally consider himself a sentimentalist or

Bristol Rovers' playing squad 1974/75. From left to right, back row: Day, Warboys, Taylor, Moore, Aitken, Rudge. Third row: Bater, Stephens, Prince, Crabtree, Eadie, Sheppard, Lewis, Britten, Coombes, Williams. Second row: Campbell (trainer-coach), Parsons, Stanton, Jacobs, Fearnley, Staniforth, Megson (team manager), Bannister, Bryn Jones, Dobson, David John, Malcolm John, Wayne Jones (physiotherapist). Front row: Powell, Evans, Pulis, Northam, Guscott.

Battle of the rival captains as former Eastville favourite Mike Green and Stuart Taylor contest possession during the Plymouth League Cup tie.

recall former glories, but he did admit to a twinge of nostalgia when he returned to Wednesday, the club he had spent all of his football career with, apart from Rovers. The match-day programme welcomed back 'The Don of Hillsborough' together with former Wednesday servants Warboys, Fearnley and Dobson. Gordon Fearnley's visit to Hillsborough was the stuff that dreams are made of. Returning to the club who gave him a free transfer without even giving him a first-team chance, the drop from the First Division to the Third must have seemed a big one then for the former England Grammar Schools striker. However, the 1974/75 season found his old club and his present club playing in the same division and, after starting the season as substitute, was recalled for the Wednesday-Rovers clash, celebrating with a goal that gave the Eastville side a richly deserved 1-1 draw. No wonder Fearnley danced a jig of delight.

Despite the sale of captain Mike Green, the Rovers manager stuck with his successful squad. Whilst able to field a side predominately unchanged from 1973/74 and largely stable throughout the season, Rovers struggled in their first season for twelve years back in Division Two. Alan Warboys, top scorer for the club with twelve League goals, and the versatile Peter Aitken both played in every game. Yet, Warboys and Bannister, 'Smash and Grab', who had netted forty goals between them the previous season, never both scored in the same game. For an attacking partnership that had yielded so many goals – both players had scored in seven different League matches during 1973/74, both bagging hat-tricks at Brighton – this season was a great disappointment.

The following season brought little further joy and it was August 1976 before both scored in the same game again. Rovers found life difficult in the Second Division and the first two seasons ended in brave struggles for points to avoid relegation. Final League positions of nineteenth and eighteenth respectively kept Rovers up, and Don Megson introduced several young players to replace some of the experienced ones who had been successful in obtaining promotion from the Third Division. During the summer of 1975, Bryn Jones left Rovers for Yeovil Town having made eighty-nine League appearances in six seasons with the club, scoring six League goals. His final match in a Rovers shirt was the 2-0 away defeat at Hull at the beginning of March. During 1975/76 the departure of John Rudge to Bournemouth was offset by the emergence of Dave Staniforth, who scored five League goals that season. Alan Warboys scored both goals in an away victory at Fulham in September, but did not score again in the League until the final game. The 3-0 defeat at Plymouth in February proved to be the final appearance in blue-and-white-quarters for Colin Dobson, who left to become youth coach at Coventry City. Both Tommy Stanton and Trevor Jacobs left the club in July 1976. Jacobs, after three seasons with Rovers, went to Bideford Town, his final game being the penultimate fixture of the season, a 3-0 defeat at Nottingham Forest. Stanton, whose last appearance was against Fulham in January, moved to Weymouth after eight years at Eastville and 168 League appearances. Despite these departures, before, during, and after the 1975/76 season Don Megson was unable to enter the transfer market to strengthen Rovers' squad.

Throughout the 1976/77 season, there was little money available for buying new players and the players who appeared on the opening day of the season mainly consisted of the side that had won five of its final twenty-nine matches in 1975/76. Without the arrival of new faces it was going to be another long, hard season. The opening game, a 4-1 home defeat by Blackpool, set the pattern for the season despite Warboys scoring his first home goal for sixteen months. On a positive note, Rovers won their first away game, with both Alan Warboys and Bruce Bannister scoring at Cardiff in a 2-1 victory. For 'Smash and Grab', a partnership that had terrorised defences during the early part of 1973/74, this represented the first time since January 1974, two-and-a-half years previously (away at Aldershot) that both had scored in the same match.

A 5-1 win over Notts County in September, when both Dave Staniforth and the recalled Gordon Fearnley scored a brace, was the biggest victory at Eastville since October 1972. Bannister's goal in a November 3-2 home defeat by Hereford United proved to be his last for the club as the old guard from 1973/74 was dismantled.

Rovers parted company with the club's deadly goalscoring duo of Bruce Bannister and Alan Warboys. Bannister had only scored four goals in eighteen appearances and was sold to Plymouth in December in a deal which brought Jimmy Hamilton to Rovers. Warboys left for Fulham in February 1977 for a transfer fee of £30,000, having turned down a move to relegation-threatened West Ham. By the season's end, after Jim Eadie joined Bath City, only Peter Aitken, Gordon Fearnley, Lindsay Parsons, Frankie Prince, Dave Staniforth, Kenny Stephens and the ever-reliable Stuart Taylor were left from the promotion season. At least the season finished on a high note with Rovers finishing in fifteenth position. Gordon Fearnley was loaned to the Canadian club Toronto Metros in May 1977 – his appearance away at Wolves on 5 April in a 1-0 defeat turned out to be his last for Rovers prior to his contract being sold to Fort Lauderdale Strikers. With the transfer of Lindsay Parsons to Torquay United on 30 July 1977, after 358 League appearances in fourteen seasons, Megson's Marvels had all but gone.

Bruce Bannister is transfer listed.

Fortunately, the following season Megson made the significant signing of non-League striker Paul Randall, together with an experienced partner in Bobby Gould, signed in October to assist the young Randall. As the season unfolded Megson entered the transfer market in search of additional players to bolster the side. However, Rovers sustained an incredible 9-0 thrashing from Tottenham Hotspur at White Hart Lane later in October, one of the eventual promotion clubs. On 21 November 1977 an era ended with the departure of manager Don Megson, who unexpectedly left Rovers to take over at Portland Timbers in the North American Soccer League. Despite having his critics whilst managing the club, Don Megson's contribution in establishing Rovers as a sound Division Two team should not be forgotten; his managerial record bears testament to that.

COMPETITION	PLAYED	WON	DRAWN	LOST	F	A	POINTS
Football League	234	80	75	79	293	304	235
FA Cup	11	3	3	5	12	19	
League Cup	19	6	6	7	24	25	
Gloucestershire FA Professional Cup	5	2	1	2	8	7	
Watney Cup	5	4	0	1	5	2	

Promoting from within, Rovers quickly appointed Bobby Campbell as caretaker-manager, whose loyalty to the club was exceptional. Campbell had come to Rovers in May 1962 originally as the trainer-coach and was asked to take over following Don Megson's seemingly abrupt decision to fly off to America in search of a more lucrative soccer livelihood. Bobby's coaching skills were sound, strong enough for that unorthodox tutor Malcolm Allison to once invite him to join him at Manchester City. Morale was low and playing ability suspect when the fifty-five-year-old Scot was given, maybe to his surprise, full managerial status.

When Megson packed his bags, the club was one off the bottom of the Second Division, seemingly rudderless at that moment. In fact, it had taken some time for the directors to decide Campbell had a potential managerial future. Twice in the past they had overlooked him when it came to promotion, but the fledgling boss, at first self-conscious about the upgrading, immediately

Bobby Campbell leaves the visitors' dugout at the end of the final game of the 1977/78 season. Bruce Bannister, then with Hull City, shakes hands with former teammate Peter Aitken.

checked the decline. Campbell's first home game in charge was on 3 December for the visit of Hull City, which included the familiar strikeforce of Bannister and Warboys. The match ended in a 1-1 draw with Dave Staniforth scoring for Rovers, but neither 'Smash' nor 'Grab' netted against their former club.

Don Megson was soon back at Eastville attending a reserve game in December with other American team chiefs, looking for players. He returned to England planning to make five signings for the start of the North American Soccer League programme, and one player Megson wanted for Portland's squad was Rovers' young defender Graham Day, who had already played for the Oregon club. In January, Bobby Campbell was appointed manager of Rovers on a permanent basis.

As fate, and the fixture list, would have it, the last match of the 1977/78 season was a visit to Boothferry Park, a match Rovers needed to win to stave off relegation. Bannister was again in the Hull side, in his familiar No. 10 shirt, but this time his striking partner was on the substitutes' bench, disgruntled with the decision to omit him from the vital game against his former club, although he did come on in the second-half. Rovers managed a 1-0 victory over an already relegated Hull City, thus guaranteeing Second Division survival for another season.

In the end, in the manner of professional football, a few critical murmurs could be heard and it was Campbell's turn to go in December 1979. The boardroom politics at the time upset the uncomplicated Scot and Campbell found himself making way for Terry Cooper, another international of proven soccer skills. At the end of the 1980/81 season Rovers finished bottom of the table with twenty-three points, winning only five games from forty-two matches, and duly returned to Division Three after seven seasons in the higher league. The only slight consolation for Rovers fans was that local rivals City were also relegated, finishing one place above Rovers in twenty-first place. It was their second relegation in succession on their way to their unique record-breaking three consecutive relegations.

MEGSON'S MARVELS

PETER AITKEN came into the Rovers side during the 1972/73 season, playing twenty-seven matches in the back-four. Born on 30 June 1954 in Penarth, he played whilst at school in Cardiff for Rovers' Welsh nursery team Clifton Athletic and Cardiff Boys, and also had trials for the Welsh Boys side. Coming to Bristol straight from school at the age of fifteen, he joined Rovers as an apprentice, signing full-time forms on his eighteenth birthday. He won nine Welsh youth caps and three Welsh Under-23 international caps against England and Scotland (twice) in 1975/76. Aitken made his Rovers debut on 29 August 1972 in the 2-2 home draw against Chesterfield, and he managed to establish himself in the Rovers team at the end of the promotion season following the loss of form by Mike Green, being an ever-present in Rovers' first season back in the Second Division.

A determined and hard-working defender, Aitken made 234 League appearances (four as substitute), scoring three times during his eleven-year association with Bristol Rovers, from schoolboy to apprentice to professional. Following a contract dispute he was transfer listed and having spent short trial periods with Watford and Blackburn Rovers, he eventually joined local rivals Bristol City in 1980. In 1982, with the Ashton Gate club in danger of folding, Aitken was one of the so-called 'Ashton Gate Eight', eight players who agreed to terminate their contracts in order to save the club from liquidation.

Peter Aiken, Rovers' Community Manager since 2000, photographed April 2010.

While at Rovers he had a spell as club captain, and after joining City he became the only footballer to captain both Bristol clubs. Aitken completed forty-one appearances for the Robins, scoring one goal, before a transfer to York City, playing eighteen times and scoring twice before the end of the season. He then had a brief spell in Hong Kong before joining non-league Bath City in July 1982. However, he left almost immediately to join AFC Bournemouth, but after one game was back at Twerton Park. He remained with Bath, making over 100 appearances, until June 1985 when he left to join Trowbridge Town at the end of the 1984/85 season. He spent three seasons at Frome Road, where he also began coaching, and then moved on to Forest Green Rovers. His second spell at Bath City, commencing in February 1988, lasted just six months and nine games and Aitken was released at the end of the season.

He returned to Bath for a third time in the 1991 close season as assistant manager under Tony Ricketts, but was released as part of a cost-cutting process before the end of the season. Peter returned to Bristol Rovers in 2000 to work as their Community Scheme Manager, a post he still holds in 2010.

BRUCE BANNISTER, born on 14 April 1947 in Bradford, played for Grange Grammar School, Bradford Boys and Yorkshire Boys. He also should have had an England Schoolboys' trial but was deprived of the chance by an untimely bout of influenza. Although born and bred in Bradford, Bruce began his career with Leeds United on associate schoolboy forms and played in their junior teams as an amateur until he was sixteen. He found that the travelling was interfering with his studies so he joined Bradford City in June 1963. Following the completion of his A-Levels he signed professional forms for the club in August 1965.

Amazingly, he was on the transfer list for the whole of the 1970/71 season during a drawn-out dispute over his contract. After more than 200 games and sixty League goals for the Bantams, Bannister moved to Bristol Rovers on 5 November 1971, manager Bill Dodgin paying a fee of £23,000, a club record at the time. Making his debut shortly after signing in a 2-1 home defeat by Rotherham United, Bannister quickly became an Eastville favourite, scoring thirty-seven League goals in his first two seasons with the club, and eighteen League goals in the successful 1973/74 campaign.

An astute penalty taker, Bannister became Rovers' leading goalscorer for three of the six seasons he was with the club, enjoying a productive partnership with fellow Yorkshireman Alan Warboys. Bannister made 206 first team appearances (four as substitute) for the Pirates between 1971 and 1976, scoring eighty League goals, before a surprise transfer to Plymouth Argyle for £10,000 plus Jimmy Hamilton.

Bruce Bannister, Managing Director of sportshoes.com.

Seven goals in twenty-four League appearances for Plymouth was followed by a further twenty goals in eighty-five games for Hull City. He was reunited with his old striking partner Alan Warboys at Hull, where the pair were joint top scorers in season 1977/78 with seven goals apiece. Sadly, when they paired up again at City they did not enjoy similar levels of success as Hull finished bottom of Division Two that season and were relegated to the Third Division. After over 500 Football League appearances and 167 goals, Bannister finished his playing career in France with USL Dunkerque (Union Sportive du Littoral de Dunkerque) based in the commune of Dunkirk, appearing for the club between 1980 and 1982.

During his career Bannister was a leading figure in the players' union, becoming a member of the Professional Footballers' Association National Executive for ten years. Bruce is now a successful businessman in Yorkshire operating a sports shoe and clothing business.

JEFF COOMBES, born on 1 April 1954, was from the Rhondda Valley and held Welsh schoolboy and youth caps. One of several Welsh schoolboy internationals who were coached by Stan Montgomery at Rovers' nursery team situated in Cardiff in the late 1960s, he joined Rovers as an apprentice and became a full-time professional in April 1972. Coombes made his Rovers debut at Eastville on 2 December 1972 in the 5-1 defeat of Scunthorpe United, coming on as substitute after the half-time interval for a 45-minute appearance. He also played in Rovers' final two League fixtures against Charlton and Chesterfield, from which Rovers picked up three points, and in the Gloucestershire FA Cup Final against Bristol City in 1972/73. Coombes made one appearance in the promotion season, playing in midfield in the 1-1 draw with Rochdale at Eastville on 5 March 1974.

The following season he made seven Second Division appearances, scoring his only League goal for Rovers in a thrilling 4-3 victory at Oldham Athletic. He also played in two FA Cup ties, both against First Division opposition; a 2-1 victory at Blackburn Rovers followed by a 2-0 defeat at Derby County early in 1975. A talented, ball-playing midfield player, Coombes never quite fitted in at Eastville and failed to establish a regular place for himself in Rovers' starting line-up. He eventually lost his place to the experienced Wilf Smith and after only fourteen first-team appearances in three seasons, left Eastville for his local club Ton Pentre in the Welsh League. His last appearance in a Rovers shirt was on 1 February 1975 against Norwich City at Eastville in a 1-0 defeat. Jeff's son, Gregg, also joined the professional ranks, signing for Cardiff City, but did not make a first-team appearance with the club. The midfielder represented Wales at Under-17 and Under-19 level and played for Oxford United (on loan), Carmarthen Town, Clevedon Town and Bridgend Town.

COLIN DOBSON, born on 9 May 1940 in Eston, Yorkshire, signed amateur forms for Sheffield Wednesday while serving his apprenticeship as an engineer, becoming a part-time professional at seventeen and a full professional at twenty-one when he moved to Sheffield. Dobson made his League debut in Wednesday's 1-1 draw with Arsenal in a First Division game at Hillsborough in September 1961. He made his name playing on Sheffield Wednesday's wings at the same time as Don Megson was their captain and left-back, spending five years at Hillsborough and winning two England Under-23 caps against Denmark and Yugoslavia in 1961. On the 22nd October 1962, in front of 49,058 Hillsborough spectators, Colin Dobson and Don Megson played for Sheffield Wednesday against Santos of Brazil, which was Pelé's first match in England. The score was 4-2 to the Brazilian champions, with Pelé scoring a remarkable penalty. However, Dobson's first-half penalty was saved by twice World Cup winner Gilmer in the Santos goal. Dobson scored fifty-two goals in 193 games for the Owls, but found himself out of the side before the 1966 FA Cup Final.

He joined Huddersfield Town for £20,000 that same year, stayed six years at Leeds Road, with the winger being a key man in Ian Greaves' 1969/70 Second Division title-winning team. The flame-haired winger made 173 appearances for the Terriers and scored fifty-two Town goals, including nine in 1969/70, having top-scored in both 1967/68 and 1968/69. Dobson scored in the 1968 League Cup semi-final first leg, which was lost to Arsenal. His last appearance was against Stoke in an FA Cup fourth-round replay stalemate at Leeds Road in January 1971. In the summer of 1968, he was selected for the Football Association Commonwealth tour of the USA, New Zealand, Malaysia and Hong Kong. Having been loaned to Brighton & Hove Albion for a month in January 1972, where he broke his leg, Dobson joined Bristol Rovers at the end of that season.

He arrived at Eastville as player-coach, linking up with Don Megson again in the summer of 1972, turning down offers from many other clubs. Dobson made his debut on 24 November 1972 in a 0-0 draw at Southend United, but an ankle injury the following February forced him to devote

Colin Dobson, still involved in football scouting for Stoke City.

more attention to the coaching part of his job in his first season with Rovers. Dobson brought many years of experience with him to Eastville and became a key member of Rovers' promotion side. He left the Pirates in 1977 to become the youth coach at Coventry City, having made sixty-two League appearances in four seasons, scoring four goals. Dobson acted as Port Vale's coach on a voluntary basis from December 1983 to March 1984, and later became coach of Bahrain and then Qatar side Al Rayyan, leading them to the championship of the United Emirates League before returning to England to take up a youth coach position at Aston Villa. He also served as youth coach at Portuguese side Sporting Lisbon, youth coach and chief scout at Gillingham and as a coach back at the Coventry City youth set-up before taking up the position of first-team coach of Kuwaitee Al Arabi.

In September 1995 he returned to Port Vale as a temporary coach, but departed in May 1996 for Oman as their national youth coach, leading the Under-17 team to win the 1996 Asian Cup in Thailand. Colin left Oman in 1999 and following spells at Stoke City and Watford, he returned to Stoke as a scout, where former Rovers teammate John Rudge is the Director of Football, and Tony Pulis, a product of Rovers' successful youth scheme, is manager of the Premier League club.

JIM EADIE, born 4 February 1947 in Alexandria, Dunbartonshire, played for Dunbartonshire Juniors as a schoolboy, for Kirkintilloch Rob Roy, the famous junior club, and then had two seasons as a part-time professional with Glasgow Rangers, playing in the reserve side, but he never made a first team appearance. Given a free transfer by Rangers he moved to Dumbarton FC in 1967, where he played a handful of matches, returning to Kirkintilloch for six months before being signed by Cardiff City. Eadie represented Scotland at Under-18 level three times and once in the Under-23 side. However, it was not until his move south in 1969 to play in the Football League that Eadie began to play regular football, although he did not make his Cardiff debut until the following year, in March 1970, when he kept a clean sheet in a 2-0 win over Portsmouth.

    The following season he managed to oust Frank Parsons as the number-one goalkeeper as Cardiff just missed out on promotion. Eadie played in sixty senior games for the Bluebirds, the most memorable being in the Bernabeu Stadium against Real Madrid in the European Cup Winners' Cup. The home tie had been won 1-0, but Cardiff were beaten 2-0 in Madrid. Following a poor spell he was loaned to Fourth Division Chester in 1972, who wanted to sign him permanently, but he was refused permission and returned to the Welsh club.

Jim Eadie at his Kingswood home, April 2010.

Signed on a free transfer from Cardiff, Eadie joined Rovers in February 1973, taking over from the injured Dick Sheppard. He made his debut on 17 February in a goalless draw at Blackburn Rovers and was nominated as man of the match. Unbeaten in his first five games for the club, he hit the headlines when he played 687 minutes of first-team football without conceding a goal, a feat which placed him top of ITV's 'Safe Keeping' League for the 1972/73 season. The following season Eadie, a big figure in goal, kept clean sheets in twenty-two of the forty-six League games as Rovers completed an incredible thirty-two-match unbeaten run in League football. Eadie, earning the affectionate nickname 'The Flying Pig' from the club's fans, spent five successful seasons with the Pirates, playing over 200 senior games (missing only three League matches) before losing his place to Martin Thomas at the start of the 1977/78 season. Following a contractual dispute with Rovers, he was set to hang up his gloves but the thirty-one-year old was tempted out of retirement by manager Brian Godfrey to join Bath City in the Southern League for the 1978/79 season.

However, a back injury limited him to just five games and he quietly disappeared from Twerton Park. Ever the character, Jim is still recognised by Rovers fans in the Kingswood area of Bristol where he now lives, still following with interest the fortunes of the club.

GORDON FEARNLEY, born on 25 January 1950 in Bradford, Yorkshire, played for Bradford Schools and England Grammar Schools Under-18 team, prior to joining Sheffield Wednesday as a full-time professional at the age of eighteen after taking A-Levels at school. Failing to make Wednesday's first team after two seasons, he was given a free transfer. Asked by former Wednesday skipper Don Megson to join him at Eastville, he arrived at Rovers in July 1970 for a two-month trial. After proving his fitness and ability he was offered a full contract, making his debut against Barnsley in a 3-0 home win in March 1971. Fearnley failed to win a regular place in Rovers' line-up at first and picked up the title of 'supersub' due to the amount of time selected as substitute. However, his introduction to a game could always be relied on to make an impression.

During the 1973/74 season he made ten full appearances, plus six as substitute, contributing three goals; he was also an unused twelfth man on fifteen occasions. Following promotion to Division Two in 1974, Fearnley finally won a regular place but failed to score goals on a regular basis. In 1977, Rovers initially sent him on loan to Toronto Metros-Croatia of the North American Soccer League, but after just one game, he was sent south to Miami Toros.

Gordon Fearnley, now resident in Florida.

Having made ninety-five League appearances, plus twenty-six as substitute (and a Rovers club record fifty-five times as an unused substitute in the 'one sub' era), scoring twenty-one goals, Rovers sold his contract to Fort Lauderdale Strikers, where he made twenty-two appearances and scored two goals. In May 1978, Fearnley was hired as the head coach of Birmingham Bandits, a team in the newly created American Super Soccer League. However, financial irregularities prevented the league from ever beginning operations and Fearnley was released. During the few months he worked with the Bandits, he met Alaina Jones, the team's Director of Public Relations, and the two eventually married. In the autumn of 1978, Fearnley left the NASL and was hired as Head Coach of Cleveland Force, of the newly established Major Indoor Soccer League, but resigned after one season and moved to Chicago Horizon.

After retirement from football, Fearnley studied physiotherapy and law in the 1980s, graduating from law school in 1991. Having set up home permanently in the United States, he left the law profession after a year to return to nursing, providing therapy and nursing services in southern Florida. Gordon returned to Bristol in May 1990 to play in a Vaughan Jones testimonial game.

MIKE GREEN, who earned high praise for both his captaincy and his consistent play in defence during the promotion season, was born on 8 September 1946 in Carlisle. He began his career as an apprentice with hometown club Carlisle United, turning full-time professional in September 1964. Green played only two League games for the Cumbrians, both the following season, before he asked for a transfer and was given a free one by Carlisle manager Tim Ward, moving to Gillingham in July 1968. He soon found a regular place at the Priestfield Stadium where he spent three seasons, playing 132 League games, scoring twenty-four goals, before another free transfer resulted in a move to Eastville in the summer of 1971.

Green made his Rovers debut in the back-four at Wrexham on 4 December 1971 in a 1-1 draw. Mike never had a settled position – playing in attack, full-back, centre half – and came to Eastville as a striker, but was successfully converted into a defender midway through his first season with the club. It may come as a surprise to Rovers fans that one of Mike's football disappointments was not playing up front more, stating in a match-day programme during the 1973/74 season, 'I enjoy scoring goals and was happy banging them in for Gillingham', where he was top scorer for two seasons.

A strong tackler, he was a member of the team which beat Sheffield United to win the Watney Cup in August 1972 and registered his first League goal for Rovers in the 2-0 victory over Wrexham in September 1972. Following the departure of Brian Godfrey, he was appointed captain

Mike Green, captain of the promotion side, now lives in the
Torquay area.

of the Eastville side at the start of the 1973/74 season, appearing in forty-four League games as
promotion was secured. In July 1974, after two goals in 77 games, he moved to Plymouth Argyle
for a fee of £19,000. Green captained Argyle to promotion from Division Three at the end of his
first season at Home Park, going on to play 108 League games, scoring eight goals.

   He left for local rivals Torquay United in March 1977 as player-manager for a fee of £5,000.
Working with the experienced Frank O'Farrell as the general manager, he put together an
attacking side at Plainmoor but could never get them challenging for promotion, not helped by the
lack of funds at his disposal.

   Green retired from playing in 1979, after eighty-eight League games and seven goals, to
concentrate on his managerial duties. During the 1979/80 season he surprisingly turned down
an offer to manage Second Division Bristol Rovers to remain at Plainmoor, but was sacked in May
1981 after a disappointing season with O'Farrell taking over as team manager for a third time.
He subsequently played for local non-league sides Newton Abbot and Hele Rovers in the 1980s.
Following his retirement from football, Mike ran a post office for twenty-two years in the Torquay
area, where he still lives.

TREVOR JACOBS was the club's only newcomer to the promotion side following his summer transfer from Bristol City. A Bristolian, born on 28 November 1946, Trevor was a prolific scorer for Bristol Boys and signed for local rivals City straight from school as an apprentice outside-right. He was released after breaking his ankle, but continued playing as an amateur, switching to right-back. He re-signed as a professional with the Robins in July 1965, making his debut in a 3-3 draw against Rotherham United, playing 130 Second Division matches (plus one as a substitute) for the club over eight seasons until being released in 1973.

His last season at Ashton Gate found him at Plymouth Argyle for a loan period that included four appearances for the Pilgrims, and he was on the point of joining Hereford United when Don Megson stepped in to sign him on a free transfer in May 1973 as a replacement for Phil Roberts, who had joined Portsmouth at the end of the 1972/73 season. Jacobs' first appearance for Rovers was against West Ham in the Watney Cup, making his League debut in the 3-0 win at Bournemouth

Trevor Jacobs pictured in Ashton Park, April 2010.

on the opening day of the 1973/74 season, and he did not miss a match in his first season with the Pirates. A renowned hard-tackling full-back, both his defensive and attacking influence in the team was significant and culminated in promotion for Rovers from Division Three as runners-up. After three years with the Pirates, making eighty-two appearances and scoring three goals – all scored in the promotion season – Jacobs decided in 1976 to retire from the professional game. His final game for Rovers was in the 3-0 away defeat by Nottingham Forest in the penultimate League fixture of the 1975/76 season. Joining non-league Bideford Town on a free transfer, moves to Paulton Rovers, managed by former Rovers' stalwart Bobby Jones, in 1977 and Clevedon Town in 1982 followed before he retired fully from the game.

In 1983 Jacobs returned to Rovers to help coach the associate schoolboys and in 1992 again assisted Rovers by coaching their South West Counties team. Trevor, a regular attendee at functions for ex-Rovers and ex-City players, is a postman in Bristol.

MALCOLM JOHN, born 9 December 1950 in Nantymoel, near Bridgend, played for Nantymoel Boys Club, Rovers' Cardiff nursery side, Clifton Athletic, and then for Rovers as a youth while still at school. He turned down the chance to become an apprentice, preferring to stay on at school to get A-Levels in history and economics before going on to college in Swansea, taking a business-studies course, and also playing as an amateur for Swansea City Reserves. He returned to Eastville after two years when Rovers offered him full professional terms on leaving college in July 1971.

There was difficulty between Rovers and Swansea over his registration, but it was eventually resolved at a cost to Rovers. He made his first-team debut on 4 April 1972 at home to Notts County, scoring the winning goal at Halifax four days later, but was then left out because Rovers were committed to pay Swansea a match fee every time he played. Malcolm made two appearances during the 1973/74 promotion season in the home fixtures against Blackburn Rovers and Huddersfield Town, scoring the winning goal in the 2-1 victory against the Terriers. He also made one substitute appearance, replacing Colin Dobson against Walsall at Fellows Park, and was named as substitute on five other occasions, but was not used.

Malcolm John, now a keen tennis player.

Malcolm joined Northampton Town on loan just before the transfer deadline in March 1974, becoming a permanent member of their playing staff the following season having made five appearances for the Eastville club. While on loan the Welshman scored four times in thirteen League appearances, making a total of forty-one appearances for Northampton and scoring eight goals before eventually returning to his native Bridgend, where he played for his hometown club in the Welsh League. In August 1975 he was transferred to Barry Town in the Southern League, playing alongside his younger brother, David, who had spent a season with Malcolm in Rovers' reserve side in 1972, but he never played for Rovers' first team.

In October 1975, after two appearances and one goal for Barry, Malcolm moved to Lewistown, and eventually retired from football due to a knee injury. Malcolm now resides in Flintshire, North Wales.

BRYN JONES, a Welsh Under-23 international, lost his first-team place through injury at the beginning of the 1973/74 season, having played in the opening three League games and the cup ties against Hull City and Bournemouth. Born on 8 February 1948 at Llandrindod Wells, he played for the Welsh Schoolboys against England and as an amateur for Cardiff City before becoming a Ninian Park apprentice at the age of fifteen, turning professional at eighteen. His League experience was limited to three appearances and after playing a few cup games for the Bluebirds, where he had a sample of European Cup Winners' Cup football against Torpedo Moscow at Ninian Park, Bryn was loaned to Newport County for two months during the 1968/69 season, playing in thirteen League matches. Released by Cardiff on a free transfer at the end of that season, he rejected offers from Fulham and Newport to join Rovers that summer, his friendship with Phil Roberts influencing his decision. He made his debut on 30 September 1969 in a 3-0 home win against Tranmere Rovers. By December 1969 he had become a regular in Rovers' midfield and scored the first League goal of his career in a 5-2 victory over Bournemouth in February 1970.

The talented midfielder, an accurate passer of the ball, won one Welsh Under-23 cap whilst with Rovers, against England in a 0-0 draw at Wrexham in December 1970; Wayne Jones and Phil Roberts also played for Wales that night. Bryn was substitute for the 1-0 victory over Finland in Helsinki on 26 May 1971, the match marking the only full international appearance of teammate Wayne Jones. The following season he lost his place to the emerging Frankie Prince, but he was a member of the Watney Cup winning side, scoring Rovers' final spot kick in the penalty shoot-out.

Bryn only played in four League games as Rovers won promotion in 1973/74, scoring in a 1-1 draw with Grimsby Town at Blundell Park, but he also made an appearance in the Nottingham Forest cup tie, replacing Colin Dobson, and was the unused substitute in the League fixture against Charlton at The Valley. Jones managed only a handful of games for Rovers in the Second Division and was transfer listed having made eighty-four League appearances (plus five as substitute), scoring six goals, for the club. In 1975, Jones became one of three summer signings by Stan Harland, Yeovil Town's new player-manager, joining former Rovers' centre forward Dick Plumb at Huish Park, playing in the Premier Division of the Southern League. In fifty-five games (plus one as substitute) in all competitions with Yeovil between 1975 and 1980, Jones scored five goals, making appearances in the Southern League, Alliance League and Conference League. Bryn retired from football in 1980 and now lives in Weston-super-Mare.

GERRY O'BRIEN, the skilful midfield player, was signed on loan from First Division Southampton by Don Megson just before the 1974 transfer deadline. Gerry was born on 10 November 1949 in Glasgow, and from school football joined Drumchapel Amateurs before signing for local club Clydebank in May 1968. He gained an amateur youth international cap against Wales. At Clydebank, he was only a part-time professional but was spotted by Southampton's scout Campbell Forsyth. O'Brien was also attracting interest from Coventry City and Nottingham Forest so the Saints manager, Ted Bates, travelled to Glasgow himself to watch him play in a 1-1 draw with East Fife in 1970. Bates liked what he saw and signed O'Brien that same evening for £22,500, then a record for a Scottish Second Division club.

He made his Division One debut at The Dell on 11 March 1970 in a 1-0 defeat by Liverpool, replacing the injured Terry Paine on the right-wing. After a few intermittent appearances, he replaced Brian O'Neil at inside-right in December 1971 and retained his place for the rest of the season, scoring one of his few goals against Derby County on 8 January 1972 with a shot from outside the area. At the start of the next season, O'Neil regained his place and O'Brien again

Gerry O'Brien returned to his native Scotland towards the end of his career.

spent much of his time in the reserves. Signed on loan to help Rovers' late bid for points at the end of the 1973/74 season, his debut for the Pirates was in the 1-0 home victory against Wrexham on Tuesday 9 March, followed by two more appearances in the quartered shirt against Rochdale and Southport. He returned to Southampton for the start of the 1974 season, appearing in a 3-0 victory over Rovers in Division Two in February 1975 and in a League Cup tie seven months later when Rovers beat the Saints 1-0. In seven years with Southampton, he made a total of ninety-six appearances, scoring three goals.

In March 1976, he was offered a move to Swindon Town and accepted what he described as 'a good offer' from manager Danny Williams. However, the move to Swindon was not a great success, O'Brien missing a lot of games due to a cartilage injury. In August 1977 he was given a free transfer back to Clydebank, appearing in twenty-four Scottish League games, scoring once in a 2-0 victory over Partick Thistle, before finishing his career at Hibernian, quitting football in 1979 with arthritis.

After a hip replacement, Gerry became a regular golfer and, on leaving football, started a building business in Glasgow before settling in Dunbartonshire.

LINDSAY PARSONS, born 20 March 1946 in Barton Hill, Bristol, played at school in Downend for South Gloucester Boys and was spotted while playing for New Cheltenham in the Church of England League by former Rovers stalwart Jackie Pitt. He signed as an apprentice professional with Bristol Rovers on leaving school in 1961 and signed his first professional contract on his eighteenth birthday in 1964. He made his debut for Rovers a month later at home to Notts County in a 4-0 win, when he stood in for Gwyn Jones. A fast, hard-working, strong-tackling defender, Parsons played at left-back despite being naturally right-footed. Parsons played in 167 consecutive League matches between 1970 and 1974, appearing in all fifty-six first-class games in 1971/72 and all fifty-seven the following season.

A Watney Cup winner in 1972, he missed only four League games as Rovers won promotion in 1973/74. Granted a testimonial the following year, Parsons remained at the club and was appointed captain in 1976. He stayed with Bristol Rovers until July 1977, sixteen years after he originally joined the club, making 354 League appearances, plus six as substitute (415 senior appearances in total) without scoring a goal. However, he was noted for his numerous remarkable goal-line clearances to stop Rovers conceding goals.

Lindsay Parsons, chief scout at Stoke City for Tony Pulis.

Turning out for Rovers' first team in fourteen consecutive seasons, his final game for his hometown club was in the last fixture of the 1976/77 season in a 2-2 home draw against Bolton. His only other Football League team was Torquay United, for whom he made fifty-six appearances between 1977 and 1980, choosing to rejoin former Rovers defender Mike Green at Plainmoor despite an offer from Northampton Town, managed by another former colleague, John Petts. From there Parsons went on to play for a number of non-League teams in the West Country – Taunton Town, Gloucester City (leading them to a Southern League Cup Final against Wealdstone), Forest Green Rovers, Yate Town, Frome Town (who he also managed) and Hanham Athletic, finally hanging up his boots in 1990 at the age of forty-four. Parsons took his first coaching job while still playing non-League football, training Bristol Rovers' schoolboy teams between 1983 and 1988.

He later gained employment as a coach at Cheltenham Town in 1990, and after Ally Robertson vacated the manager's position in 1992 Parsons was appointed to the position in a caretaker's capacity. He was later given the job permanently, achieving some success before leaving to join Gillingham as assistant manager in the summer of 1995. Parsons forged a strong working relationship with his former Bristol Rovers teammate Tony Pulis, working with him in various coaching and scouting capacities at Gillingham, Bristol City, Portsmouth, Stoke City, Plymouth Argyle, and at Stoke City again from 2007, where he is currently chief scout.

FRANKIE PRINCE, born on 1 December 1949 in Penarth, South Wales, played as a youngster with Leeds United's Terry Yorath for Cardiff Central Boys Club before joining Rovers' highly productive South Wales nursery. He signed associate schoolboy forms for Bristol Rovers at the age of fourteen, becoming an apprentice professional in 1964 and earning his first professional contract in December 1967, aged eighteen. Prince made his Rovers debut at home to Swindon Town in April 1968, a game Rovers lost 2-1. He enjoyed many good times with Rovers in the League Cup, being a member of the teams which reached the quarter-finals in two consecutive seasons, 1970/71 and 1971/72. The following season they reached the fourth round by defeating Manchester United at Old Trafford in a sensational 2-1 giant-killing victory. A tremendously competitive player who, besides his ball-winning qualities, could pass accurately, Prince was a member of the Rovers team which won the Watney Cup; his goal at Burnley in the semi-final of this competition was featured in the BBC video *101 Great Goals*.

Frankie Prince became Torquay United's Football Community Officer in 1992.

Two bone fractures in 1972/73 hampered his progress, but he recovered to play a leading role in the Third Division promotion success. Prince played four times for the Welsh Under-23 team, was substitute for the full international against England in Cardiff in 1972 but did not make it off the bench, and in 1971 accompanied Rovers' teammates Wayne Jones and Phil Roberts on a Welsh FA tour of New Zealand. A hero of the Eastville terraces, Prince went on to make 362 League appearances and score twenty-two goals in a thirteen-year spell with the Pirates before joining Exeter City in 1980 on a free transfer. There he played a further thirty-one League games and scored two goals. Following the end of his League playing career in 1982, Prince had spells at non-League clubs Gloucester City, Taunton Town, Ottery St Mary, Bideford Town and Clyst Rovers.

Following a break in his football career, during which time he worked for eighteen months as a nursing assistant at Dawlish Hospital, Frank returned to professional football when he joined Torquay United in 1992 as their 'Football in the Community' officer, setting up the club's Community Scheme.

JOHN RUDGE joined Bristol Rovers from Torquay United in February 1972 as a striker in a part-exchange deal with Robin Stubbs. He highlighted his goalscoring ability in his first full season at Eastville by scoring in both epic League Cup ties against Manchester United. Born on 21 October 1945 in Wolverhampton, John became a Huddersfield Town apprentice at the age of fifteen and a professional two years later, making his debut against Swansea Town during the 1962/63 season. Second Division Huddersfield were a mid-table side in 1963/64, coming close to promotion in 1964/65 and 1965/66, but with Rudge still a young player learning his trade, he made only five League appearances between 1963 and December 1966. He found regular football at Second Division rivals Carlisle United between 1966 and 1968, scoring sixteen goals in fifty League games before joining Third Division Torquay United in 1969, where he became the club's leading goalscorer. Rudge stayed with the Gulls for three seasons, switching clubs after relegation in 1972 having scored thirty-five goals in ninety-five League games. During 1969/70 and 1970/71 he was the club's top scorer with sixteen and twenty goals respectively.

Rudge made his Rovers debut on 26 February 1972 in the 2-1 home win over Walsall, and made fifty League appearances (plus twenty as a substitute) for the Pirates, scoring seventeen goals

John Rudge, Director of Football at Stoke City since 1999.

during four seasons with the club. His playing career was ended at the age of thirty-two in 1977 due to an Achilles tendon injury after a three-year spell with Bournemouth. They had suffered relegation to the Fourth Division in 1974/75, and Rudge scored twice in twenty-one League games for the Cherries.

Following his retirement as a player, Rudge joined the coaching staff at his old club Torquay United, managed by former Rovers teammate Mike Green. In January 1980 he was appointed as a coach at Port Vale, and in the December was promoted to the position of assistant manager under John McGrath. Following the sacking of McGrath in December 1983, Rudge was made caretaker manager, but was unable to prevent relegation that year. He went on to manage the club for a sixteen-year period between 1983 and 1999, easily the longest spell in the club's history. The 1988/89 season was highly successful, Port Vale beating Bristol Rovers 2-1 on aggregate in the two-legged Division Three play-off final, and for the first time in thirty-two years Vale reached the Second Division. Rudge managed his team to Wembley twice in 1993, winning the Football League Trophy Final 2-1 over Stockport County, but losing the play-off final 3-0 to West Bromwich Albion. He masterminded some of the club's most successful ever campaigns, but was sacked in January 1999 having been at the helm for 843 Port Vale games.

Following this, he was made Director of Football at rivals Stoke City, where he is currently working. When the club achieved promotion to the Premier League in 2007/08, Rudge was at a top-flight club for the first time since entering the game forty-eight years earlier in 1962.

DAVE STANIFORTH was signed for £20,000 from Sheffield United just before the transfer deadline in March 1974. Born on 6 October 1950 in Chesterfield, he played for Nottingham County Boys from the age of twelve to fifteen. In 1966 he was offered the chance to join Huddersfield Town, but he rejected it in order to continue his education. Spotted by Sheffield United and signed as a junior, he became an apprentice professional before joining the full-time ranks with the Blades in 1968. Staniforth got into the first team at the age of eighteen, playing twenty-six First Division games and scoring three times before being signed by Rovers.

He made his Rovers debut in the 2-1 home win over Huddersfield Town on 9 March 1974 and played in a total of eleven games (three as substitute) and scored two goals (the winner against Wrexham in the 1-0 victory and the opener in the 2-1 win over Aldershot) in the final push for promotion. He also scored one of the goals in the 2-0 end-of-season triumph over Bristol City in the Gloucestershire FA Professional Cup Final at Ashton Gate. For six consecutive seasons Rovers were able to benefit from his strength and ability, despite him initially playing in the shadows of

Dave Staniforth, a support officer with South Yorkshire Police.

Bannister and Warboys. A consistent and reliable forward, he was made Rovers' club captain in November 1977 following the appointment of new manager Bobby Campbell. Staniforth made 135 League appearances (plus sixteen as substitute) and scored thirty-two goals for the West Country side during a five-year stay at Eastville.

Bradford City signed him in 1979 for a fee of £24,000, for whom he scored twenty-five goals in 107 appearances (plus eight as substitute). His seven League goals during the 1981/82 season helped them to win promotion from the Fourth Division. He then moved to Halifax Town as player-coach in 1982, and the following season was voted Halifax Town Supporters' Club player of the season. Halifax proved to be his final club, for whom he appeared in sixty-six League games (plus three as substitute), scoring twenty-one goals. Dave retired from full-time professional football in 1984, joining Burton Albion in the Northern Premier League where he scored at least five goals. He also went into partnership forming a building company which he ran for twenty-one years.

On the retirement of his business partner in August 2005, Dave decided to close the company and seek an alternative career, joining South Yorkshire Police in September 2005 as a support officer, a role he thoroughly enjoys mostly because of the diversity of the tasks.

TOM STANTON, born on 3 May 1948 in Glasgow, became a Scottish Schoolboys international and signed amateur forms for Liverpool, turning professional in 1965 at the age of seventeen. After a year with their senior squad without playing a League match, he was released by the Anfield club. Tom spent a month with Kilmarnock before joining Arsenal in September 1966 following a successful trial there. One year later, having failed to play in a League game for the Gunners (he played in two London FA Challenge Cup ties), Stanton joined Mansfield Town after a loan period with the club. He eventually made his League debut after joining Mansfield and went on to play thirty-seven times for them, scoring once against Peterborough United in October 1967. He played in the 3-0 victory against Rovers in March 1968.

Twelve months after joining the Stags he accepted manager Fred Ford's offer to come to Eastville in the summer of 1968, making his Rovers debut on 31 August 1968 as substitute for Joe Gadston in a 6-1 drubbing at Crewe Alexandra. His first start for Rovers was at left-back on 9 October 1968 at Shrewsbury Town. At one stage in his Rovers career Stanton considered quitting League football, becoming disillusioned that he could not establish himself as a regular member of Rovers' senior side, but he decided to give himself six more months in the full-time game during

Tom Stanton, pictured in April 2010, runs a telecommunications
company.

the 1971/72 season. In 1972/73, injuries to Frankie Prince gave the Scot the chance to establish
himself as an effective midfielder after a number of seasons as a reserve full-back. An ever-present
in the 1973/74 promotion season, scoring both goals in the 2-0 victory over Halifax Town, by 1976
Stanton had played in a number of positions, including goalkeeper after Dick Sheppard had been
injured against Tranmere Rovers in January 1973. In eight seasons with Rovers he made 168
League appearances, eleven of those as a substitute, and scored seven times, before dropping
down into non-League football in 1976 when he joined Weymouth. In 1977 Stanton joined Forest
Green Rovers as player-coach, and in 1980 returned to Bristol Rovers as reserve team coach.

   Another stint as a player-coach followed in 1982, this time with Clevedon Town, where he was
later appointed manager. Stanton returned for a third spell with Bristol Rovers in 1983, where he
spent a year coaching their schoolboy teams. In 1984 he joined local Bristol club Durdham Down
Adult School. Still resident in the Bristol area, Tom now runs a successful telecommunications
business.

KENNY STEPHENS, the Bristol lad who was lured away from his home town by the appeal of First Division football, came home to make good and establish himself as an immensely popular member of the Eastville playing staff. Born on 14 November 1946, Stephens played for Speedwell School, Broad Plain, Phildown Rovers and represented the Bristol Downs League as a teenager. From school he went to West Bromwich Albion as an apprentice professional, becoming a full-time professional at eighteen. He first appeared for West Brom in a 2-2 draw with Sunderland at Roker Park in October 1966 and played in a FA Cup semi-final against Birmingham City in April 1968. After four seasons with the Baggies and twenty-two League appearances (plus one as substitute), scoring twice, he was transferred to Walsall for £15,000. A disappointing spell at Fellows Park, playing only seven League games for the club, resulted in him quitting football at the age of twenty-three for nine months and taking a job as manager of a newsagents' business in the West Midlands.

Deciding to try for a comeback, Rovers arranged for him to have a month's trial at Eastville in 1970, which led to him initially being offered a three-month contract by manager Bill Dodgin, followed by a full contract. Kenny made his debut for Rovers in the home game with Barnsley at Oakwell on 2 January 1971, scoring in a 4-0 win. The outside-right soon became a firm favourite at

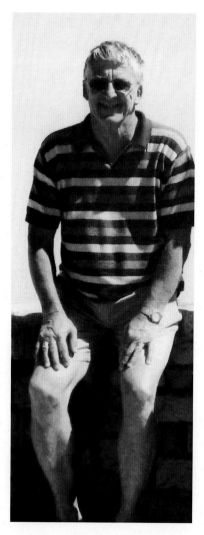

Kenny Stephens, one-time president
of local club Hanham Athletic.

Eastville, where his intricate skills and ball control were greatly appreciated. During his second season with Rovers, Stephens scored eight League goals, but the goalscoring was to dry up before long. Two years later he was a member of the side promoted to Division Two, but the goal he scored at York in March 1974, before being sent off for one of two occasions in his Rovers career, proved to be his last in the League for the Pirates.

After 215 League appearances (plus ten as a substitute) and eleven goals for Rovers, Stephens joined Hereford United in October 1978 where he made sixty appearances and scored two goals, eventually appearing in all four divisions before making his final appearance in February 1980 against Wigan Athletic. A short spell with Gloucester City then followed. Stephens has had a long association with local Bristol club Hanham Athletic, one of the founder members of the Gloucestershire County League in 1968, who in their first season finished in a respectable third position.

During the 1980s Hanham came as close as they did in 1968 by finishing third on two occasions under the managerial guidance of Stephens, who later became president of the club for a number of years. Still living locally, Kenny, a builder and decorator by trade, is involved in his brother's building business.

STUART TAYLOR, the 6ft 5in centre half who manager Don Megson rated as the best in the Third Division, was born in Bristol on 18 April 1947. Captain of Bristol Boys, after leaving school Stuart played for South Gloucestershire Boys and Abbotonians, signing as an amateur with Bristol City in 1963 whilst undertaking a plumbing apprenticeship. Released after two years with the Reds, he joined Hanham Athletic but after ten games accepted an amateur engagement at Eastville. Taylor signed as a part-timer a year later and as a full-time professional in April 1967 after making his Rovers debut the previous season, in a goalless draw at Workington on 26 April 1966. His first Rovers goal was scored against Bristol City in the FA Cup third-round replay at Eastville on 30 January 1968, which City won 2-1. Taylor established himself in the Rovers line-up in the 1967/68 season and not only was he a commanding figure in defence, he was a formidable attacking weapon too. That campaign he scored eight goals using his physical attributes and excellent timing to turn in corners and free-kicks.

The following season, he had a slightly different role. He swapped over to the No. 4 shirt to make way in the first team for a promising youngster, Larry Lloyd, forming a partnership known as the 'Twin Towers'. However, before the season had finished Lloyd was sold to Liverpool. An injury during the 1972/73 season broke a run of 207 consecutive League appearances going back to

September 1968 and, but for this, he might well have broken goalkeeper Jesse Whatley's amazing club record of 246 successive League games between 1922 and 1928. Taylor's run of appearances between 1968 and 1973 remains a post-war record for the club.

An ever present in the promotion-winning side, he was rewarded with the club captaincy the following season. A consistent and determined defender, Taylor spent his entire professional playing career at Bristol Rovers, holding the club record for most League appearances with 546 League games played in his fifteen years at the club, contributing twenty-eight goals during that period. He made a total of 620 senior appearances (thirty-eight FA Cup and thirty-six League Cup outings) and scored thirty-four goals. On leaving Rovers in the summer of 1980, Taylor was appointed as player-manager of non-league Bath City, turning down the opportunity of a one-year contract with Chelsea. After nearly two seasons at the City helm, with the club struggling financially, he turned down an offer to go part-time and was sacked in April 1982. He became commercial manager with Bristol Rovers for a brief period shortly afterwards.

Retaining a strong interest in amateur football, he saw out his playing days at Cadbury Heath and even played in goal for Bristol side Taylor Brothers in 1993. Stuart became landlord of three public houses in the Bristol area before later returning to his former trade as a plumber. Stuart continues to follow the club's fortunes, watching all the home matches at the Memorial Stadium.

Stuart Taylor outside the Memorial Stadium, April 2010, where he regularly attends matches.

ALAN WARBOYS, born on 18 April 1949 in Goldthorpe, Yorkshire, joined Doncaster Rovers as a schoolboy from West Riding junior football, later becoming an apprentice and a full professional with the South Yorkshire club, making his debut in April 1967 at the age of seventeen. He moved to Sheffield Wednesday from Belle Vue in June 1968 as a nineteen-year-old, having made forty-three League and Cup appearances, as part of an exchange deal with Brian Usher, where he made seventy-nine appearances and scored thirteen goals. Following Wednesday's relegation in 1970, Warboys joined Cardiff City for a fee of £42,000 as a replacement for John Toshack, who had joined Liverpool.

On his home debut for the club, Warboys scored twice against the team he had just left, Sheffield Wednesday, and went on to finish the season scoring thirteen goals in seventeen League games, including scoring four times in one match during a 4-0 win over Carlisle United, which included a hat-trick in the opening 9 minutes of the game. At Cardiff Warboys played alongside Jim Eadie in the Bluebirds' European Cup-Winner's Cup tie against Dynamo Berlin in 1971. He spent two years at Cardiff City, scoring twenty-seven goals in sixty League appearances, before returning to Sheffield – this time United – in the 1972/73 season as part of a swap deal which saw Gil Reece and Dave Powell move the other way to Ninian Park, but made only seven First Division appearances without scoring.

Rovers' manager Don Megson had known the striker as a youngster at Sheffield Wednesday and had tried to sign Warboys for the Pirates earlier in the season, but things had not gone well

Alan Warboys, photographed in May 2010, still regularly meets up with his former striking partner.

as the negotiations had become public knowledge. The second attempt, orchestrated by Colin Dobson, went more smoothly, Megson completing the signing before the public announcement was made. Warboys joined Bristol Rovers for a then club record fee of £35,000 in March 1973, making his debut on the 6th in a goalless home draw with Rochdale. In his five seasons at the club, he forged a lethal forward pairing with Bruce Bannister which would be much-celebrated, taking Rovers to promotion to the Second Division and earning the duo the nickname 'Smash and Grab' in reference to Warboys' physical playing style and Bannister's ability to grab the resulting chances created by him.

Transferred to Fulham in February 1977 for £30,000, after 141 League appearances (plus three as substitute) and fifty-three goals for Rovers, his short spell at Craven Cottage brought two goals in nineteen appearances, before a move to Hull City at the start of the season, being reunited with his old striking partner, where the pair were joint top scorers in season 1977/78 with 7 goals apiece. Sadly, this time the partnership was not as productive and Hull finished bottom of Division Two that season and were relegated to the Third Division. Returning to Doncaster Rovers in 1979, in his first season back at the club he was awarded the club's Player of the Year award.

Manager Billy Bremner then played Warboys in defence towards the end of his career, but he missed much of the 1981/82 season after undergoing an operation to remove a disc from his back, which forced his retirement at the end of that campaign. In a career playing in all four divisions, Warboys scored 137 goals in 479 League appearances. After retiring from football Warboys ran a pub in Swinton for eight years. Now settled in the Doncaster area, Alan, since his retirement as a publican, has driven lorries for a local haulage company.

DON MEGSON, born on 12 June 1936 in Sale, Cheshire, is regarded as one of Sheffield Wednesday's greatest servants, establishing himself both as a fine player and ambassador for the club. He was recruited by Wednesday in 1952 from Mossley in the Cheshire League, for whom he had been turning out as a left-winger, turning professional that October. In his early days at Hillsborough Megson proved to be something of a utility player, playing in most outfield positions before he became established at centre half. However, manager Harry Catterick felt that Megson had more to offer as a full-back, and that final switch of position prompted a run of form which saw him make the step up to the first team, making his debut in November 1959 against Burnley, facing England winger John Connelly. Having made that breakthrough, he quickly became a regular in the Owls' defence at left-back, his passion, enthusiasm and style making him a fans' favourite. Megson was chosen as successor to Tom McAnearney as club captain in October 1964 and skippered Sheffield Wednesday as they won away from home in every round to reach the 1966 FA Cup Final. Despite the disappointment of a cruel defeat, 3-2 to Everton, Don led the players on a lap of honour around Wembley stadium – the first losing captain to do so.

That incident epitomised the pride which Megson felt at leading the side and, indeed, no player dared give less than 100 per cent when Don was around. He twice played for the FA, captaining a touring English FA XI in New Zealand in 1969, was an England reserve in 1960, when he also played for the Football League, and won a League championship runners-up medal in 1961. Megson was an ever-present in four seasons during the 1960s and made 442 appearances (including 386 League appearances, scoring six goals) for Sheffield Wednesday before moving to Bristol Rovers as player-coach in March 1970. When Megson joined Rovers they were close to the end of the 1969/70 campaign, and missed getting into the Second Division by a mere four points.

Megson's Rovers debut came on 28 March in a 1-0 home victory over League leaders Orient. In the two seasons he played for Rovers, he made thirty-one League appearances and scored one goal, and featured in the League Cup run that saw Rovers reach the quarter-final stage, scoring

Don Megson at Bristol Rovers 125th anniversary dinner, April 2009.

a memorable goal against Norwich City in the third-round replay at Eastville. He took charge of the reserves for twelve months before succeeding Bill Dodgin as manager in the summer of 1972. Megson managed Bristol Rovers from 1972 to 1977, winning the 1972 Watney Cup in only his third game in charge and gaining promotion from the Third Division in his second season; by the time he left Eastville in November 1977 for a three-year contract with Portland Timbers in the North American Football League, he had established Rovers as a Second Division side.

Don Megson was hired as head coach of Portland Timbers for the 1978 season after Brian Tiler was unable to turn the team around in 1977. Megson was finally able to replicate the success of the 1975 season, with the team improving and qualifying for the playoffs. However, he was unable to repeat his own success and the team again struggled in 1979, and he did not return the following season. Back in England, Megson managed AFC Bournemouth for seven months in 1983, resigning after a poor run of nine defeats in eleven League games, including a 1-0 home defeat by Bristol Rovers on 27 September. He worked as a freelance scout for Bolton Wanderers, the club whom his son Gary managed, until December 2009. Both of his sons, Gary and Neil, played and managed professionally.

Megson returned to Rovers for the first time in April 2009 – he had not been back to the club since leaving in 1977 – to attend a champagne reception and dinner to mark the 125th anniversary of Bristol Rovers FC. He was amongst a number of former managers and ex-players attending the dinner at the Marriott Bristol Royal Hotel, the culmination of a year of celebrations.

BOBBY CAMPBELL, born in Glasgow on 28 June 1922, began his career with the city's Perthshire junior club before commencing his senior career at Falkirk in 1941, although the war limited his competitive seasons there to just one, 1946/47, when he scored six goals in sixteen League appearances. During the war he did service in London – where he played wartime football for Queens Park Rangers – and in India, where he served and played alongside Tommy Walker, then a Heart of Midlothian forward, who would join Chelsea in 1946. On Walker's recommendation, Chelsea's Scottish manager, Billy Birrell, bought Campbell in 1947, paying a substantial fee of £9,000. The investment was rewarded not just with Campbell's goals but the assistance he gave Bristolian Roy Bentley, Chelsea's top scorer in every season they played together. Bobby made an immediate impact for the Blues, scoring twice on his debut in a 4-2 defeat of Aston Villa at Stamford Bridge. He went on to net twelve times in thirty-four games during his first season.

Bobby Campbell belonged to the generation of great Scottish footballers who lit up pitches across Britain in the immediate post-war years. He was a quick, technically capable player whose versatility meant he could function on either flank or as an inside forward. His preference was to operate on the right, from where his crosses routinely provided goals for Bentley. Having played 213 games and scored forty goals in a seven-year stay at Stamford Bridge, he was sold to Reading in August 1954. The team he left behind, under the management of the moderniser Ted Drake and the captaincy of Roy Bentley, promptly won the First Division in 1954/55 for the first time in their history.

Campbell's five caps for Scotland – two in May 1947 and three in the spring of 1950 – fail in themselves to tell the story of why he did not win more. Scotland was blessed in that era with an abundance of talent, especially in the forward areas. Those were the days of Hibernian's 'Famous Five' forward line: Gordon Smith, Bobby Johnstone, Lawrie Reilly, Eddie Turnbull and Willie

Ormond, who all won multiple Scotland caps in the post-war years, with Smith being a direct rival to Campbell for a place in the national side. In that context, Campbell's five caps were no small achievement. His international debut, whilst still a Falkirk player, was in a 2-1 defeat by Belgium in Brussels. Retaining his place for Scotland's next match, he was then overlooked by the selectors for the next three years. An injury to Celtic's Bobby Collins saw him called up against Switzerland in April 1950, his only Scotland goal coming in the 3-1 victory in front of a capacity crowd of 123,751 at Hampden Park in Glasgow. He later said of that strike, 'It gave me the greatest thrill of my life'.

Campbell's move to Reading at the age of thirty-two, for £2,000, meant he missed out on title glory but he prolonged his playing career until he was thirty-six, scoring twelve goals in ninety-four games during four years at Elm Park. He also began a coaching career there which led, in 1961, to a year in charge at Dumbarton. Campbell left Boghead Park a year later in May 1962 to move to Bristol Rovers, where he spent fifteen years as a trainer-coach and two more as manager before being sacked on 11 December 1979. The highlights of his time as Rovers' coach were promotion to the Second Division in 1974, and before that success in 1972 in the Watney Cup, still the only major trophy success in Rovers' history. Bobby Campbell may not have been Rovers' greatest manager, as he did not hold the post for too many seasons, though his quiet influence was often apparent at dear old Eastville.

His last managerial appointment was with Gloucester City. After retiring from football, he continued to live in the Bristol area coaching unemployed youths and was a frequent spectator at home matches at the Memorial Stadium, where he remained a popular figure with fans, former players and directors alike. At Hampden Park in 2008, Campbell received a commemorative cap from the Scottish Football Association as one of the players recognised when they retrospectively overturned their pre-1975 policy of only awarding caps to those who had faced one of the home nations. Bob died on 4 May 2009 at the age of eighty-six.

Bobby Campbell and members of the promotion team, 25 April 2008. From left to right: Peter Aitken, Stuart Taylor, Lindsay Parsons, Jim Eadie, Mike Green, Frankie Prince, Alan Warboys, Bruce Bannister, Tom Stanton, Trevor Jacobs, Bobby Campbell